• THE JOYOUS GIFT OF •

grandparenting

101 Practical Ideas & Meaningful Activities to Share Your Love

▼

Doug and Robin Hewitt

hatherleigh

NEW YORK

Hatherleigh Press is committed to preserving and protecting the natural resources of the Earth.
Environmentally responsible and sustainable practices are embraced within the company's mission
statement.

Hatherleigh Press
5-22 46th Avenue, Suite 200
Long Island City, NY 11101
www.hatherleighpress.com

Library of Congress Cataloging-in-Publication Data

ISBN 978-1-57826-267-0

The Joyous Gift of Grandparenting is available for bulk purchase, special promotions,
and premiums. For information on reselling and special purchase opportunities,
call 1-800-528-2550 and ask for the Special Sales Manager.

Cover and interior design by Pauline Neuwirth, Neuwirth & Associates, Inc.

Illustrations by Beth Kessler

10   9   8   7   6   5   4   3   2   1

Printed in the United States

DEDICATION

In memory of my mother Geno Mary Peura (1922-1969), who only met three of her eleven grandchildren, yet touched the lives of them all with her love and sense of humor. Mama, I still remember The Secret Password.

For Gavin, Kenna, Jake, Alyssa, and "Number 5," for all the joy and inspiration you give us from the innocence and wisdom of your youth.

To Grace Robbel and Don and Kay Clemens, for being such wonderful grandparents to our own children; to June Adcock and Harve and Jane Hewitt, the "grandparents to the north"; to the Paduchowskis, Robbels, Shattucks, Garskas and Sticklers, with whom we share the joy of our grandparenting.

To all the grandparents who are raising their grandchildren, a special prayer of success in your great endeavor.

ACKNOWLEDGMENTS

We would like to give a special thanks to Michael and Sara (and their partners) for giving us our grandchildren; Amy, Andy, and David for the grandchildren in our future; the Writers Group of the Triad, our support group of writers that are always there with an answer or suggestion; Alyssa, for another wonderful job of editing, and the rest of the Hatherleigh team; the AARP, for their grandparenting advocacy; and Andy Webb and Kathy Sweet for all their grandparenting discussions and suggestions.

CONTENTS

INTRODUCTION:
HOW TO USE THIS BOOK

▼

THIS BOOK IS for grandparents who are seeking help planning activities with their grandchildren. Anyone involved in the raising of a child—aunts, uncles, and even siblings—will benefit from the activities, conversation starters, and advice within. Whether you see your grandchildren just once a month, weekly, or are their primary caregivers, today's world can be hectic. It's difficult to plan activities that can nurture and strengthen your family bonds while still allowing you to have fun and make those loving, lasting memories.

Grandparents are becoming more and more involved in the direct care of their grandchildren. Sometimes overworked parents will use you as a daycare facility; sometimes parents just need time to themselves; sometimes it's the financial burden that ends with the grandchild at your doorstep. For whatever reason, grandparents everywhere find themselves with pre-teen children again in the house. And grandchildren often have a lot of energy. You want to nurture them, to help them grow into loving, successful, responsible adults. How?

This book will give you ideas for activities that will rev up their imaginations, open their minds to new ideas and concepts, and develop their social skills. While participating in these activities, you'll find chances to speak with your grandkids come naturally. Each activity is paired with conversation starters: open-ended questions and topics. The ensuing conversations will lead you both to close, intimate conversations that will bond you together. Although the activities are mostly geared for children age thirteen and under, some activities, such as stargazing with a telescope, can be enjoyed by all.

If you're on a tight budget or fixed income, you'll be delighted to find that many of the activities in this book are free or no cost. And of course, simply reading the Fun Facts can be enjoyed by all! With the slim wallets and tight time constraints in this modern world, it's difficult to put together activities that are both meaningful and enjoyable—at least at first glance.

Nurturing grandchildren isn't just about activities, it's about having conversations at the same time. Grandchildren tend to open up when they're doing something with you, versus being grilled across the dinner table. The key is to ask open-ended questions. All the activities in this book are paired with a "While You're at It" section, which lists questions you can ask your grandchildren and interesting topics to discuss. It's a very practical way to help you get those bonding conversations started.

Envision a holiday get-together with the grandkids. Won't it be great when the grandchildren come in and the rounds of hugs and kisses are just the continuation of your year-long involvement with them, and a glowing tribute to the nurturing relationship you have?

While it can be easy—and tempting—to deposit the kids in front of the TV or video game station, this book will stress that the use of television should be moderated. TV can be a great way to keep the grandkids entertained while you're busy, but it's going to be hard to create those lasting memories, active discussions, and great relationships without moving off of the couch.

If you are looking for ideas for a short visit, you'll find plenty in the early chapters, designed with visitation length in mind. These chapters include "The One-Hour Stopover," "The Day Visit," and "The Overnight Visit." Further on, you'll find chapters organized by travel distances, "Short Trips" and "Long Trips," and other helpful situations such as "All Friends Are Invited!" "'Tis the Season," and "When You're Rained Out."

You might feel as if some of the activities in this book are not especially relevant to you. If you rent an apartment, for example, the activities for the yard don't apply. Still, there are parks you can visit. Be creative and use your imagination—just as you are prompting your grandchildren to use theirs.

We are sure that you'll find the practicality of the advice within the most helpful. This book presents a blueprint for what you can do to raise and nurture grandchildren, written by grandparents who love their grandchildren. Our favorite chapter is "In the Toy Trunk" because of its relevance to daily life. We keep a storage tub in the trunk of our car, and it's filled with activities for those extra 10 minutes you find here and there while waiting in the car, whether it's at a drop-off or in a traffic jam.

We believe in having open-ended, meaningful conversations with our grandchildren, but if you've ever tried to talk to a shy youngster, you understand that it's not always that easy. We hope you'll find that the techniques we've used with our children and grandchildren work for you. Participating in activities with your grandchildren can inspire you to have those open-ended conversations. Asking questions, soliciting your grandchildren's input, *conversing* with your grandchildren while working/ playing together will go a long way in helping your grandchildren grow up into mature, responsible adults.

So, browse by chapter, or read straight through, then keep the copy at hand for reference. If your grandchildren are old enough, let them read the book and suggest activities that appeal to them. Even if this book provides you with just a few ideas for nurturing your grandkids on limited time and exposure, it will be well worth your effort.

GRANDPARENTING PRINCIPLES

As grandparents, we've found that as good as these activities are, we needed to follow a set of principles to guide our actions through the nurturing process. Below, you'll find twelve principles that have worked for us, and we believe that they will work for you, too.

PRINCIPLE 1

Don't forget that you are a role model. It won't do much good to preach one thing and practice another. Grandchildren will instantly spot the hypocrisy (although they might not yet be familiar with the word). Your grandchildren will mimic what you are doing, not saying.

PRINCIPLE 2

Advise your children on what you think is best for the grandchildren, but in the end, it's important to remember that your children are the parents, not you. It's their job to do. They might resent you for using your status to try and impose your set of parenting principles on their kids.

PRINCIPLE 3

Keep in touch. It's not always easy to stay in touch with your grandchildren. People move because of employment responsibilities, and sometimes you are just very busy. But in today's world, there's no reason for not staying in touch; in addition to snail mail, there's email and telephone. Take the time to write a letter to your grandchildren. Writing is becoming such a lost art!

PRINCIPLE 4

Expand your grandchildren's horizons. Sometimes the parents can get too narrow a focus and forget to allow the grandchildren to explore new ideas and talents. Let them try new things.

PRINCIPLE 5

Don't buy your grandchildren's affection. Spending a lot of money on a grandchild can not only spoil him or her, it can also severely strain your relationship with the parents. It's a time-worn adage, but money can't buy love.

PRINCIPLE 6

Every grandchild is different. What works for one might not work for another. Some hate ketchup, some love it. And let's not get into the pickles controversy. . . .

PRINCIPLE 7

Make sure you don't laugh at or mock your adult children as they struggle with parenting. Your grandchildren will be putting them through the same pains they put you through. At least try not to laugh in front of the kids!

PRINCIPLE 8

Remember that raising children is tough. There's no single right way to raise a child successfully, and in fact no single way to define what a successful child-rearing experience is. There will be times when things

don't go the way you think they should. Hang in there. Life has a way
of balancing out.

PRINCIPLE 9

Don't criticize the parents in front of the grandchildren. The grandchildren know, at least on some level, that they are part of their parents, and so often they feel it's direct criticism of them.

PRINCIPLE 10

Never undermine the parenting that the parents are doing. Grandchildren (and all children) need routines and unchanging rules. Don't
change them. Don't tell them that something the parents have ruled
out is okay. It's better to disagree with the parents in private than to tell
the kids your opinion and undermine their parents' authority.

PRINCIPLE 11

Be a foundation of trust for your grandchildren. Never lie to them,
and don't make promises you may not be able to keep. While this
is good advice for anyone to follow, it's especially important for
grandparents who are trying to become closer to their grandchildren.
One broken promise can set you back months. If you can't trust your
grandparents, who can you trust?

PRINCIPLE 12

You are the bridge to their roots. Share your memories with your
grandchildren so they can learn from your experience and learn about
their great-grandparents and beyond. You've been through a lot in
your life. Don't hold your wisdom close to your chest.

THE JOYOUS GIFT OF
GRANDPARENTING

1

THE ONE-HOUR STOPOVER

▼

THE TELEPHONE RINGS. Your daughter or son is calling to let you know they'll be in your area and want to know if you'd like (or mind) if they stop by for an hour or so. Great! You get to see your grandchildren. But what can you plan on such short notice—and for such a short time period?

The activities in this chapter will be great for those quick, little visits. And remember, you can squeeze a lot of memories out of a short period of time.

DID YOU KNOW?

Children today spent on average more time per week watching television than attending school. The exact reason is unknown: perhaps it's the increased choices available on children's channels on television, or maybe it's because children nowadays don't have as many chores to do. In addition to the TV viewing, here's another point to consider—obesity in children has now reached epidemic proportions, according to the Centers for Disease Control and Prevention (CDC). One study suggested that children today only spend 38 minutes a week in meaningful conversation with their parents. Statistics like these should make grandparents want to make the extra effort to keep the television off, interact with our grandchildren, and have those open-ended conversations they need. Not only is it good for their health, it'll be good for yours, too!

MORE INFORMATION: BOOKS

Rao, Goutham. *Child Obesity: A Parent's Guide to a Fit, Trim, and Happy Child.* Prometheus Books. Amherst, NY: 2006.

Providing tips to help overweight kids get control of their weight, this book also provides a rational approach for combating weight gain.

Berg, Frances M. *Underage and Overweight.* Hatherleigh Press. New York, NY: 2005.

More than a diet and exercise plan, this book encourages families to promote a more active lifestyle and provide healthier food choices, rather than prescribing aerobics and limiting portions.

Thomason, Colleen, and Ellen Shanley. *Overcoming Childhood Obesity.* Bull Publishing. Boulder, CO: 2006.

The book provides useful, up-to-date information and helps with meal planning. It includes information on contemporary nutrition issues.

MORE INFORMATION: WEBSITES

www.cdc.gov

The Centers for Disease Control and Prevention website has a wonderful array of health and fitness topics and information, including information on childhood obesity.

www.surgeongeneral.gov

The Surgeon General of the United States uses this website to address public health issues, including calls for action on the problem of child obesity, and gives a good overview of the frightening statistics. Includes eating and activity suggestions.

STENCILS

Fun Fact

During World War II, the T-shirt became standard underwear issue for both the U.S. Army and the Navy.

All you need for this activity are some permanent markers, medium-weight cardboard, safety scissors, and some T-shirts. Use your imagination to cut out designs from the cardboard. It might be helpful to draw the design with a pencil before cutting. After you cut out the design, place the cardboard over a T-shirt flattened onto a table or floor. Use the marker to draw through the cut-out sections. You've just succeeded in creating a stencil and making your first T-shirt design!

Try some of these stencil ideas on for size:

► Write your names in fancy letters across your back like a sports star.
► If the T-shirt has pockets, create a small insignia over the pockets. Look in some of the clothing ads and see what logos are already used. How about a crocodile (Izod)?
► Make a line of paper-doll cut-outs.

- ▶ Make outlines of your grandchildren's hands, cut them out, then color them in. When the color is dry, the grandchildren can sign and date them!
- ▶ Make shapes based on their favorite sports or hobbies.

If you want to get fancy, get different colored markers, fabric paint, or stencils. We suggest outlining your drawing in black first. (Tip: If you use a pencil, then you can erase mistakes.) Once everybody is satisfied that the outline is good, use the black permanent marker to make it official. Then fill in the outline with different colors. Now, wear the shirts out to get ice-cream or to a sporting occasion, or store them away for birthday or holiday gifts.

A GRANDPARENT ASIDE

There are plenty of times when a parent is too busy to show up on parent-teacher days. Volunteer to take their place! It's important to be openly excited about this proposition, because the grandchildren might feel slighted by their parents' lack of participation. "Better for me!" you might tell them. And even if the parents plan to go, ask if they will agree to let you come along. It might be a good idea to tell them how much you enjoyed (and miss) going to their own teacher conferences; this will help convince them that you're not "checking up" on their parenting abilities. Understand that taking an interest in grandchildren's schoolwork will motivate them to put more work into it, and you will get to see their accomplishments firsthand. Talk to the teachers and see if there is anything you can do to help your grandchildren along. For example, the teacher might suggest that some extra reading would help, or reciting the multiplication tables. Even if you don't make it to the parent-teacher conference, attend school functions whenever you can. Your grandchildren will appreciate it.

WHILE YOU'RE DRAWING ON T-SHIRTS:

▶ Talk about logos on clothing. What are they there for? What are some that they can remember? For example, military uniforms have flags. Sports teams have team names (and sometimes the player's last name on the back) and numbers.

▶ Ask if they've seen any T-shirts like the ones they are creating at their school. Are they allowed at their school?

▶ Have the kids ask their parents for ideas on whom to give T-shirts to.

▶ Ask to have them work together on a special T-shirt for you for a present.

PAPER FOOTBALL

Fun Fact

A football is called a pigskin, but it is actually made of leather from a cow's skin.

This easy-to-play, easy-to-plan game can be done as easily at a restaurant's table as it can be in the house. To create your football, cut a sheet of paper in half, fold the top corner down and across to the other side, forming a triangle. Continue folding the top corners down, alternating sides, until you reach the bottom of the paper. Tuck away any excess paper into the pocket formed by the folds. (If you're at a restaurant, use the paper from a straw.) Sit opposite your grandchild at a table and flick the triangle across the surface of the table. If any part of the triangle is hanging over the edge of table, it's a score. Falling off the table is out of bounds and awards no points. Try taking turns to see who can get the most points in a row. You can also use this "ball" to play paper hockey.

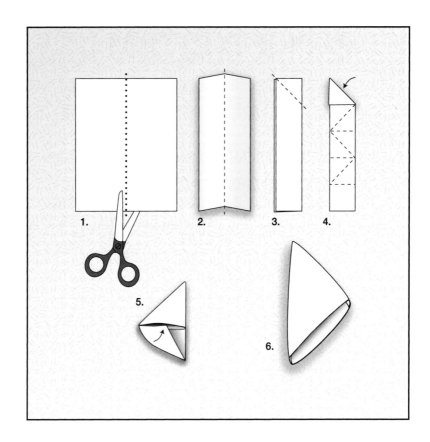

1. Cut a sheet of paper in half lengthwise.
2. Fold corner down into triangle.
3. Continue folding triangles for length of paper.
4. Tuck rectangle excess into the "pocket" on top of the triangle.

A GRANDPARENT ASIDE

Raising children nowadays often happens with many generations involved, from the grandparents to the parents and the great-grandparents.
Helping your children raise your grandchildren to be moral, responsible, and successful adults can be tricky. Sometimes advice can be seen as

interference, so it's good to find a middle ground. A good way to give advice without lecturing is to use a non-threatening approach, such as "Do you think they might respond to _____?" or "It might be a good idea to try _____." Another key to remember is that advice is always taken more readily when it follows praise, such as "You're always so patient and quick-thinking!" You want to be listened to, not ignored. Sometimes parents have to feel their own way through a sticky situation. When you sense resistance to an idea you try to put forward to the parent, decide if this is an issue that you really need. It's best to "pick your battles" and possibly even wait until you are asked for advice. It's true! Take it from us—a couple of "battle-tested" grandparents.

WHILE YOU'RE PLAYING PAPER FOOTBALL OR PAPER HOCKEY:

▶ Explain how a "bank shot" works (ricochets), and how it can help them score.

▶ Try a silly trick to distract them while you attempt to score. (Our favorite is "Look, there's Elvis!")

▶ Try flicking the paper triangle with different fingers to find a finger that works best.

▶ Why are there referees in sports games? If the paper football is near the edge of the table, who makes the judgment call on whether or not it's a "score?"

STATIC EXPERIMENTATION

Fun Fact

Static electricity buildup is so high on top of the Empire State Building that, under the right conditions, if you stick your hand through the observatory fence, a glowing electrical aura will stream from your fingertips.

Even if your grandkids aren't science whizzes, experimentation on how things work is sure to intrigue them. One of the simpler ways you can spark their interest is static experimentation. All you need to do is to rub a balloon across a sweater. Place the balloon carefully by a wall (preferably painted and not wallpapered) and then see if it will stick. Dry conditions are best, so if the weather is very humid, this might not work. It often works best to give them the visual aid (a balloon stuck to a wall) and then do the research for the explanation. Electricity is a good thing for grandchildren to learn about, especially its dangers. While children might know not to stick their fingers in electrical outlets, it's better if they understand why it's so dangerous.

Once you've piqued their interest, sit them down to find more information online about static electricity and charges. If they're young, you can relate it to the charges on a magnet. Magnets won't give you a shock, though, and static electricity will. If you want to get fancier, there are science kits available that can have experiments running in under an hour.

A GRANDPARENT ASIDE

Let's talk about communicating with your grandchildren. Have you ever heard that most of communication is nonverbal? With animated grandchildren like ours, there's not only communication going on—it's like a fun-filled variety show. Seriously, though, if you don't have eye contact with your grandchildren while they're talking to you, they might unconsciously think that you are not listening as attentively as you could be. Who knows—maybe their parents are so busy that they don't have time to listen for minute after minute (after minute . . .) of how the kid's day went. And it's important! Occasionally repeat what your grandchildren say to show them you are listening closely. Ask questions for clarification. Show interest in what your grandchildren have to say (nonverbally as well as verbally), and they will develop interesting things to say.

WHILE YOU'RE LEARNING
ABOUT STATIC ELECTRICITY:

▶ Talk about why some electricians in the Navy are nicknamed "Sparky."

▶ Explain the dangers of a static discharge near a gasoline pump. Ask your grandchildren to read the warning labels on the pumps and report back to you on their next visit.

▶ See if you can rub a balloon on their hair to make it stand up.

▶ Talk about how "grounding" something keeps charges from building up, which explains why some vehicles such as forklift trucks have straps that drag along the floor.

NERF BALL

Fun Fact

Because of the shape of the ball, Chinese often call American football "Olive Ball."

A game of football can be played with any number of grandchildren. We recommend our version of this game because everyone switches positions after a few plays. This mixes up team members, and so if there's an age difference, any advantage that older children have gets evened out. In a football setting, there's a passer, a receiver, and a defender. After each snap of the ball, the receiver runs out into the field and tries to catch the pass. The defender tries to block or intercept the pass. We suggest that everybody takes a turn to play three times each as passer, receiver, and defender. Both the passer and receiver earn one point for a catch; the defender gets one point for an interception. Usually, we get so involved that it's difficult to remember the score, but who cares about that when you're having so much fun?

A GRANDPARENT ASIDE

If everything they wanted or needed was handed to them on a silver platter, it would be difficult for your grandchild to be humble, fair, or selfless. Keep this in mind when the grandchild reels into a round of "I want that!" There was a time when our grandchildren seemed to think that every store we went into was a candy store, and . . . , well, if you've ever seen a kid in a candy store, you know what we mean. Still, while it's definitely your right to spoil your grandchildren, keep it in moderation. A grandchild needs to recognize early that there are things that need to be earned, and that they can get satisfaction from the earning as much as the actual receiving of the item. This can go a long way in helping a child understand that making one's way in the world involves more than just asking for things.

While you're playing three-person Nerf ball:

> ▶ Talk about ways to play the game better. How about trying to "fake out" the defender by pretending to want to go left when you're going to go right?
> ▶ What's the Heisman Trophy? (A trophy awarded to the college football player voted the best by sports analysts.)
> ▶ Do they care about who wins? Why? Point out that many professional athletes never win a championship and are still considered winners in their communities because of all of their relief work and community service.

BOWLING

Fun Fact

Although we bowl with 10 pins in the US, other countries have different rules. Canada plays with 5 pins, and Europe with 9.

Set up your own bowling alley in your back yard by using milk cartons, 2-liter soda bottles, plastic jugs, or anything that will stand upright. Have the kids scrounge around for ideas. For the bowling ball, use a beach ball, baseball, or bouncy ball. The object here isn't to exactly recreate a bowling alley, but instead to just have something that resembles one. Because everybody will be playing with the same ball and pins, the game will be fair. We suggest having a notebook and pen at hand to keep score, especially with those pesky spares and strikes. If you're unsure about how to score a game of bowling, check online with the kids. If your grandchild is old enough, assign him or her the task of learning the rules of scoring and then ask for them to explain it to you. There are also inexpensive bowling sets made from plastic that are available at toy stores. Everyone should take turns at setting up the pins after they're knocked down.

A GRANDPARENT ASIDE

Although there are plenty of golden grandparenting opportunities available from the comfort of a lounge chair or when standing beside the kitchen counter, sometimes the best way to interact is by playing with your children outside. Where is your grandchild's world? Helping to expand their world outside can be a wonderful step in the development of the grandchild. For example, while planning for an excursion to a gem mine, we took our grandson Gavin (age 5) outside. It was the day before our trip, and we asked him to help us decide what we needed to bring. What would help us get gemstones out of the ground? We came up with lots of good ideas. The next day, as we set out on our two-hour drive to the mine, Gavin grinned and exclaimed, "I've been waiting for this my whole life!"

WHILE YOU'RE BACKYARD BOWLING:

▶ Ask how many times a week your grandchildren would like to bowl if time and money were no object.

▶ Would they like to watch a professional bowling tournament on TV?

▶ Explain how the gutters in a bowling alley resemble gutters on a house.

CLOTHESPIN SAILBOAT

Fun Fact

What large American city has a huge sculpture
of a clothespin in its downtown area?
(Philadelphia)

Some of your grandchildren might not even know what a clothespin is, so start this activity by explaining it to them. Once you get some wood clothespins, you will have to remove the springs, then glue the flat sides of the wood together, creating boat hulls. For the sails, poke toothpicks though small squares of paper. Glue the toothpicks into the spring holes in your hulls. Poke small colorful paper triangles onto the top of the toothpicks for flags. Add weights so they stay upright. (Try using a hot glue gun and gluing pennies on the bottoms of the hulls.) You can paint the clothespin in all kinds of fun patterns!

Blow them around in the bathtub or take them to a park and race them down a creek. Remember that creeks can be dangerous for young (and old) folks, especially if the current is swift. If you choose to do this, look around for reports of recent rainfall or snow melt. The number of children drowning each year is a somber reminder of how dangerous water can be.

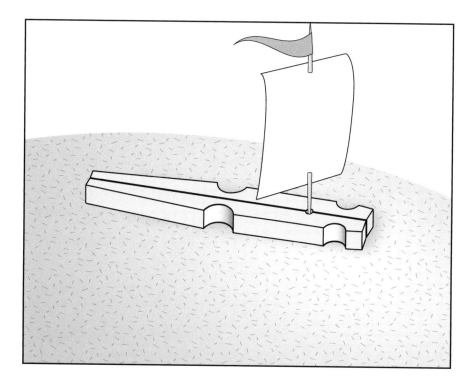

1. Remove spring from clothespin.
2. Glue flat sides together.
3. Place toothpick in spring hole, set with dot of glue.
4. Poke square of paper onto toothpick for sail.
5. Poke small triangle onto toothpick for flag.

A GRANDPARENT ASIDE

Safety can never be overstressed. Many workplace slogans reflect the saying: Safety Is Job #1. Why should it be any different with our grandchildren? So, along with other reminders of safe practices, such as keeping seatbelts buckled, take the time in every activity you do to remind your grandchildren of the risks involved with it. For example, in a clothespin boat race, there's a risk of drowning. Run them through an example, and ask them to hold their breath. Time them. Then, explain that if their heads are under water, they won't be able to breathe. Speaking of breathing, for us it's breathtaking the way our grandkids can come up with ways to stretch the limits of being safe. We always try to stay one step ahead by playing mental recordings of us saying, "I wonder what they're up to now?"

WHILE YOU'RE CONSTRUCTING
AND SAILING YOUR CLOTHESPIN BOATS:

▶ Talk about how people sailed their boats long before the invention of motors and engines.

▶ What are the disadvantages of a sailboat? (No propulsion when the wind dies, unless there were oarsmen.)

▶ See if there's some item of clothing they would like to hand wash and then hang out to dry with a clothespin.

▶ Come up with fun names for your clothespins.

LAWN TARGETS

Fun Fact

There are 3,000 blades of grass in each square foot of an average lawn.

This low-cost activity can be hours of fun. Create a circular target from a piece of string or rope. We suggest a circle about three feet across—the size of a Hula Hoop is perfect! Then, step back from the target to a distance determined by the ages of the grandchildren and try to toss your "ammo" into the circle target. You can use nearly anything (bean bags, coins, even paper airplanes). Score three points for being completely in the circle, two points for being partially in the circle, and one point for being within a foot (or some other distance that everyone agrees on) from the edge of the circle. Play ten throws each, and the high score wins. If the game goes quickly, have a tournament in which there are 10 games, and the player with the most game victories wins the tournament.

A GRANDPARENT ASIDE

We've talked to many grandparents over the last few years who spoke about what's important to them. Many of them want to leave the world a better place than when they entered it. What better way to accomplish this than by having their grandchildren motivated to contribute to the world's well-being? Grandparenting is a great way to feel as if you have accomplished wonderful things during your stay on Earth. We would argue that there's no job more important or satisfying. And as this book can attest, we try to have as much fun as we can doing it!

WHILE YOU'RE PLAYING LAWN TARGETS:

▶ Ask if they've ever played a game of darts. Are they old enough to hold something with such a sharp point?

▶ Why is it important to stretch muscles before physical exertion? (It helps prevent muscle strains and other problems.)

▶ Have them try both underarm and overhand throws. Compare results and see which works best. Point out that attempting different techniques to see what works best is a good habit to develop in life.

JOKES

Fun Fact

The "Knock Knock" joke format has been around since at least 1953.

If you are a natural storyteller, this is an activity you may already be doing. When your grandchildren come over, sit down with them and discuss some types of stories that exist. For example, a story that illustrates a moral lesson, or some lesson of life, like Aesop's fables. Remember the story of the ant and the grasshopper? The ants worked all summer, storing food, while the grasshopper played. Come winter, the ants had food, the grasshopper didn't. It illustrates how important it is to think and plan ahead. Talk this over with your grandchildren and see if you can come up with your own stories. For bonus points, have them volunteer to tell the story at their school or child care center.

A GRANDPARENT ASIDE

For us, Grandpa Doug and Grandma Robin work just fine. But what do your grandchildren call you? Gramps and Grams, PawPaw and Nana, Grandpa and Grandma? Whichever names they are, this might change if you suddenly become a full-time caregiver. This name is between you and your grandchildren; while the parents have a right to express their opinion, your name should be your decision. Parents can and sometimes do object to certain names; often there is a request from another grandparent for a specific title, and the parents get stuck in the middle.

If you are the primary caregiver of an eight-year-old, the grandchild might feel more comfortable calling you Ma or Mom in social settings. Keeping the lines of communication open is very important, so if they want to fit in with the names they use at school and when they are with their friends, oblige.

WHILE YOU'RE COMING UP WITH A STORY:

▶ Talk about Aesop and how these fables taught lessons before the advent of school textbooks.

▶ Teach them the word "didactic," which means meant to teach a lesson or provide instruction. What are some other interesting words having to do with language?

▶ Have them watch the president give a State of the Union speech and see if the president uses a story to make a point.

THE DAY VISIT

▼

WHILE AN HOUR with your grandchildren will give you enough time to connect, having the entire day provides many more opportunities to do things together. You'll find activities in this chapter that require a good chunk of the day. Sometimes, because of time constraints, it can be difficult to spend an entire day with a grandchild. We all have chores to do, bills to pay, appointments to keep. Still, spending an entire day with a grandchild can create memories that will flourish in their minds into bonds that will last forever, and the laundry won't go anywhere!

Sometimes these opportunities come along when the parents "need a babysitter" for a day because they have something they need to do without the children. If so, great! If not, you might want to volunteer to "babysit" while they take a day for themselves to spend some quality time with each other.

If you pick the grandkids up at their house for the day, you'll get the added bonus of spending time with them in the car, when you'll be able to catch up on their activities since you last saw them. Having them dropped off at your house works well, too, because the grandchildren will have a growing sense of anticipation during the drive over and will be excited when they see you. Either way, everybody wins!

DID YOU KNOW?

When we were younger, SIDS (Sudden Infant Death Syndrome) was referred to as "Crib Death" and seemed to be quite rare. A parent would go to wake up the baby, which would be found dead for no apparent reason. Now the medical field has a better understanding of the causes and risks, and there are preventive measures that can reduce the chances of a baby falling victim to SIDS.

SIDS is far from rare; up to 6,000 children annually die from it. If you, or anyone you know, is caring for an infant and is unfamiliar with the latest medical advice, take the time to find out what you can do to save a life. Three simple things to keep in mind: always place infants on their backs to sleep, use firm mattresses, and don't overheat the rooms. It's always a good idea to talk to a pediatrician. In the meantime, find out more using the resources below.

MORE INFORMATION: BOOKS

Parker, James N., and Philip M. Parker. *The Official Parent's Sourcebook on Sudden Infant Death Syndrome: Directory for the Internet Age.* ICON Health Publications. San Diego, CA: 2005.
This book covers a wealth of SIDS topics and includes Internet resources to guide you to the latest information available.

Levene, Malcom I. and Mary Rudolf. *Paediatrics and Child Health.* Blackwell Publishing Limited. Malden, MA: 2006.
This is a British textbook on common clinical presentations of diseases and disorders in childhood. It includes sidebar summaries of key points.

Fries, James F., Robert H. Pantrell, and Donald M. Vickery. *Taking Care of Your Child: A Parent's Illustrated Guide to Complete Medical Care.* Da Capo Press. Cambridge, MA: 2005.

This book covers more than 75 common pediatric healthcare problems and symptoms, addressing probable causes, seriousness, and possible at-home treatments.

MORE INFORMATION: WEBSITES

www.sids.org

The American SIDS Institute's website. This nonprofit health organization has helpful information to reduce the risk of SIDS and a good links page.

www.sidscenter.org

The National SIDS/Infant Death Support Center's website has helpful information, useful links, and an excellent Frequently Asked Questions page.

www.sidsalliance.org

The SIDS Alliance's website provides information to help infants survive and thrive their first year, with help for families who have lost a child to SIDS.

FISHING

If your grandchildren are very young, you can spark their interest in fishing by creating a fishing hole at home. First, plant some metal fishes in a tub (try using washers). Then, tie a magnet to a string, attach the string to a pole or stick, and send them off on a fishing trip. Later, you can buy or borrow real fishing gear and go see what you can catch. (Fishing licenses might be required; check with your state wildlife department if you're not sure about the legal restrictions.)

Even if you're in a populated area, you'll find lots of places to go fishing. In many areas, there are stocked ponds on private lands where no license is required, and you're almost certain to catch something! As a bonus, if there's not a history of pollution (such as mercury) in your area, you may be able to clean the fish and have a fish dinner.

A GRANDPARENT ASIDE

It's not too difficult to see that in the future, people will have less and less a connection to the food they eat. While some people today opt to be vegans or vegetarians, in the past this wasn't always an option. Survival once depended on finding food to eat (such as fish to catch). There are many people today who have never seen an animal such as a chicken, cow, or pig outside of a petting zoo. In the future, people might not even see a corn stalk, let alone a hog that is being prepared for bacon-making. As a ketchup-loving family, we want to point out that this isn't just pointing out the similarity of the color of tomatoes to that of ketchup (although we've done that). We're suggesting that it's not a bad idea for you to introduce your children to where food comes from, perhaps by taking a trip to a neighboring farm.

WHILE YOU'RE FISHING:

▶ Talk about how fish are cold-blooded, which means their body temperature is the same as the water they are in.

▶ Are there any fish-like creatures in the oceans that are mammals (warm-blooded like humans)? (yes)

▶ Can you name a mammal of the sea? (dolphins, whales, and porpoises)

▶ Are there vegetarian fish? (Yes; some fish, such as the parrot fish, eat only algae, which is a plant.)

F
I
S
H
I
N
G

PHOTOGRAPHY

Fun Fact

Some states in the Midwest have a hunting season for bullfrogs!

When it's time for a nature stroll or a wildlife hunt, stop by the drugstore and buy each of the grandchildren a one-use camera. There are two reasons: if there are any accidents, they will not result in the loss of anything expensive, and having their own camera will make them feel as if they are real photographers. Now, take the grandchildren out and see what kind of wildlife you can find. It can be unusual plants, colorful flowers, birds, dogs, or cats. Be creative! Then drop the camera off to be developed. On the next visit, you can present your grandchildren with the pictures and even make a photo album of your wildlife hunting adventures together.

A GRANDPARENT ASIDE

If you have a computer in the house, consider keeping it in a centralized area. This way, whenever the grandkids want to use the computer or find something on the Internet, you can keep an eye on their activities without appearing as if you are, or having to go out of your way. It's always a good idea, too, to talk about what they are looking at on the Internet. It's also a good idea, whether or not you have a computer, to know what your grandchildren are up to. We keep a shortcut to the Nickelodeon website on our computer's desktop so the grandkids can play safe online games that we approve of (www. nick.com/games).

WHILE YOU'RE HUNTING WITH A CAMERA:

▶ What are some of your grandchildren's favorite photographs?

▶ Would they like to take a picture of a friend?

▶ What kind of animal or plant would they most like to take a picture of?

▶ Why is a picture worth a thousand words? (A picture conveys information like colors and shapes that would take a lot of words to describe)

TROPICAL FISH STORE

Fun Fact

A pregnant goldfish is called a "twit."

You don't have to buy anything. You can spend hours just looking at the fish and aquarium accessories, and the children will be thoroughly entertained. While you're watching the fish, talk about the fish (or pets) you had when you were a child. Tropical fish are typically very colorful and eye-catching. This can be a wonderful afternoon at no cost. Our grandchildren will spend hours just looking at the various kinds of tropical fish.

Note that we recommend visiting a fish store rather than a general pet store because of the animal abuse that is perpetuated by many of these stores, such as placing exotic parrots into cramped cages that can deform them for life. Of course, animal abuse should be reported to local animal shelters and national animal welfare associations (visit www.aspca.org for more information).

A GRANDPARENT ASIDE

There are many instances, especially when they're younger, when grandchildren (and children in general) feel like nobody loves them. That's when you can be there for them the most, and be the support system they need. We aren't suggesting that you should say your grandchildren are always right or that they should never be disciplined. We believe, though, that children can have rough days, just like adults, and there are times when knowing Grandma and Grandpa love and support them will help them. Think about it like a small kid striking out his or her first time at bat when trying out for T-ball. Are you going to express disappointment? Of course not! You're going to say, "What a great swing! You'll get a hit next time!" This way, grandchildren will understand that loving grandparents are rooting for them to succeed.

WHILE YOU'RE AT
THE TROPICAL FISH STORE:

▶ Do the grandkids have any questions for the fish store employees on how they care for the fish?

▶ What are the costs of owning an aquarium?

▶ Talk about how much time is required to care for fish and compare to the time for different pets such as cats and dogs.

▶ Think up some potential names for different types of fish based on their looks. It might be good to mention how the equivalent for nicknames for humans is sometimes cruel (i.e., fatty).

BIRDHOUSE

Fun Fact

There are a total of 86 North American birds that are cavity nesters (who might use birdhouses).

Imagine how wonderful it would be to build a birdhouse with your grandchildren and spend the entire spring and summer seasons watching birds nest and their hatchlings grow up and learn to fly. Take pictures and create a photographic journal of the process. When it's time for the nuts and bolts, search online or visit the library with the grandkids. If you go online, try your favorite search engine (ours is Google) and search for birdhouse building projects. For a simpler approach, many craft stores and toy stores provide kits that usually require only the minimal tools like a hammer and a screwdriver or two. Of course, you'll want to paint and decorate your birdhouse. Discuss with your grandchildren what kind of birds they'd like to attract—the size of the entry hole makes a difference!

A GRANDPARENT ASIDE

As with children, grandchildren need ground rules. If they're visiting you for more than a day (or especially if they live with you), they'll want to expand their time outside of the house, and as they grow older, they will want to spend time visiting their friends. It's important to have curfew times. Of course, as they grow older and approach their teenage years, the curfew time can be extended. Negotiate with your grandchildren on the time and the penalties for missing curfew. Ours are still too young to even be thinking about driving licenses, so we're anticipating revisiting this subject in the years ahead.

WHILE YOU'RE MAKING A BIRDHOUSE:

▶ Why is a nest important? (to protect the bird's eggs)

▶ See if you can find the picture of an eagle's nest online. Do your grandkids know the name of an eagle's nest? (an aerie)

▶ Does your birdhouse have shingles? Why do shingles help protect the wood from water damage? (Shingles keep the wood dry so it won't rot)

BOOKSTORE TRIPS

Fun Fact

During the 18th century, books that were considered offensive were sometimes punished by being whipped.

Most bookstores have children's sections that are designed to delight your grandchildren. You can spend hours browsing through books with your grandkids and let them play with the toys available. If your grandchildren are still small, sit down and read a few picture books to them. What kind of book interests them the most? There are fewer gifts better than a book, and it's a great way to spend time together! Our personal tradition after a bookstore trip is to have lunch at a nearby deli. We spend the mealtime talking about books we bought (or wanted to) and sometimes the people we saw at the store and what books and magazines they were browsing . . .

A GRANDPARENT ASIDE

There are going to be different (or more) rules to follow at your house than your grandchildren may be used to following at their own home. Perhaps there are rooms off limits to them. You might have special cabinets with breakable china or other commemoratives. Maybe you have a rule against snacking. Different rules are okay (within reason, of course) as long as they are carefully explained to the grandchildren. One of the best ways to make sure the grandchildren understand the ground rules is to have them repeat the rules in their own words. And again, as with any rule, it's often best to explain what the punishment will be. This can be a carrot and stick approach. In our house, Doug likes to break the ice with the "stating of the rules" by opening with his overly serious golden rule #1: Grandpa Doug gets dibs on his chair when the game's (usually football or basketball) on TV.

WHILE YOU'RE AT THE BOOKSTORE:

▶ See if there's a bargain book section. There are often large "coffee-table" books with lots of wonderful, large pictures. See if your grandchildren are interested in any of these.

▶ Ask if your grandchild would like to write a book. Encourage them to try! Maybe they can illustrate it themselves, or get a friend to lend a hand.

▶ Get your grandchild to impress you (and you obviously must act impressed) by having him or her read a few sentences to you aloud.

GREETING CARDS

Fun Fact

The first commercial Valentine's Day greeting cards made in the U.S. were created in the 1840s.

When it's nearing time for a special occasion (whether it's a birthday, Mother's Day, or Father's Day), take your grandkids on a fact-finding trip to your local pharmacy or card store. You can get some ideas for cards by browsing through the greeting card sections there. Talk about whose birthdays are approaching. Do you need a reason or a holiday to give someone a card? Maybe somebody just needs to be cheered up, or perhaps somebody is recovering from an illness. Now, instead of purchasing a card, pick up the materials to make your own at home (construction paper, markers, glitter). What a wonderful opportunity to have a memory-making day with your grandchild!

A GRANDPARENT ASIDE

Alert! Grandchildren will push boundaries. Yes, we're sure you knew this from your own parenting days, but it's worth mentioning in a book like this. They might take it easy on you, the grandparents, but kids will be kids. They might want you to buy something that the parents have expressly forbidden, or listen to CDs at your place that they aren't allowed to at their home. They may think it's unfair in the first place, which is why they think they have a right to instill some fairness back into their life and not be totally honest with you. This may not be an issue with your grandkids. However, it's a good idea to be alert and stay in contact with the parents. Make sure everyone is on the same page when it comes to boundaries.

WHILE YOU'RE MAKING CARDS:

▶ Is there a special event in your grandchild's life that they remember well?

▶ Ask what they'd like on their next birthday.

▶ Discuss how much fun it is to get a letter delivered via snail mail. What are some of the best parts of this? (anticipation at opening the envelope)

WALKIE-TALKIES

Fun Fact

The first radio receiver/transmitter to be nick-named "Walkie-Talkie" was the backpacked Motorola, created in 1940 for war use.

This project is simple to make and gives you and your grandchild your own secret way of communicating. Just poke small holes in the ends of cans and connect them with string. Make sure the cans have no sharp edges. Frozen-juice cans work well. Use short strings at first to test the range of your distant communication devices. Try them around the corners of different rooms, or try to slip the string under a door. It works very simply: one person talks into one of the phones, while the other person holds theirs up to an ear to listen. It will work best when the string is stretched tightly.

A GRANDPARENT ASIDE

You probably remember when newspapers were the primary source of news. We saw somewhere recently (probably in a newspaper) that the majority of people in the U.S. now get their news online. There is nothing wrong with this; however, there's a certain amount of charm that goes into taking Sunday morning going over the Sunday paper from back to front with your grandchildren. It'll be fun! We're sure there are sections that your grandchildren never knew existed. Try the crossword puzzle with them. If you don't understand sudoku puzzles, have your grandchildren figure it out and show you. There are cartoons to laugh at, movie reviews to peruse, and current events to learn about. So, pour some orange juice, grab some donuts or bagels, and sit down with your grandchildren.

WHILE YOU'RE MAKING WALKIE-TALKIES:

▶ Talk about telephone wires. You can see them all along the sides of roads everywhere you go; how do they carry electric signals that carry the signals our voices make? (Telephones change our voices into changes in current in the phone line, which are transmitted to other telephones, which in turn change the current fluctuations into voices.)

▶ Talk about yodeling. This was a long-distance form of communication developed in the Swiss Alps. Different sounds, pitches, and tones were used to communicate different signals.

▶ What's the difference between how land-line phones and walkie-talkies work? (phones via an underground cable or the telephone lines, walkie-talkies via batteries)

3

THE OVERNIGHT VISIT

▼

WHETHER IT'S AT their place or yours, the overnighter offers plenty of opportunities to bond with your grandchildren that aren't available with the daytime visits. For example, you're able to tuck them in to sleep and say, "See you in the morning." You're able to greet them with a hug when they wake up. The overnight visit is an important step to take that helps to cement the bonding process with your grandchildren. During some point in your grandparenting career, you'll no doubt find yourself the primary caregiver, when every day comes with an overnight visit. Good for you! This can be challenging, and having gone through the parenting process once already makes it more than a little tiring, but the rewards are there in the end.

The activities in this chapter were chosen because of the unique opportunities that overnight visits present.

DID YOU KNOW?

While the average temperature of the human body is 98.6 degrees Fahrenheit, everybody's body temperature will fluctuate during the day. Typically, body temperatures are lower after first waking up the morning. Children lose body heat more readily than adults, which is a risk for infants in cold weather because of their inability to shiver to generate heat. Activities such as running and playing can raise body temperature. Check with your doctor or the grandchild's pediatric doctor if there are any questions about what can be considered normal when checking a grandchild's temperature.

MORE INFORMATION: BOOKS

Children's Hospital Boston, Berry T. Brazelton, and Alan D. Woolf. *The Children's Hospital Guide to Your Child's Health and Development.* Perseus Publishing. New York: 2002.

This is a very comprehensive book, coming in at 816 pages. It includes sections covering developmental stages and addresses many health issues.

The American Dietetic Association. *Play Hard, Eat Right: A Parent's Guide to Sports Nutrition for Children.* Chronimed Publishing. Minneapolis: 1995.

As the title suggests, especially good for the active and athletic children.

Tamborlane, William. *The Yale Guide to Children's Nutrition.* Yale University Press. New Haven, CT: 1997.

This book answers many questions regarding nutrition and is well researched. It also includes healthy recipes!

MORE INFORMATION: WEBSITES

www.kidshealth.org/parent

This is an excellent website for finding information related to children, including health, nutrition, medical and behavioral issues, and more.

www.webmd.com/a-to-z-guides/Body-Temperature

This provides a good overview of body temperature, explaining such things as the difference between oral and ear temperature readings.

www.ds-health.com/fever.htm

This provides good information about fever in children and it can be quickly read.

FLASHLIGHTS

Fun Fact

The flashlight was invented in 1898, and "Let There Be Light" was printed on the 1899 Eveready catalog to advertise their newest product.

The world feels like a different place at night. Going out at night into the yard with flashlights can illuminate an entire "new" world for your grandchildren. It can also ease any latent fear of the dark they might harbor. It's a good idea to make sure the flashlight works before heading out, and carrying extra batteries or a spare flashlight can be smart, so you won't be caught out in the dark. If you live in a well-lighted neighborhood, maybe you can visit relatives with yards not quite so brightly lit.

Try some of these activities with flashlights:

▶ Play ghost tag. If the light from a flashlight spots you, you're "it."
▶ Play hide-and-seek.
▶ Go to a beach and chase "ghost" crabs!
▶ Hold the flashlight under your chin and make monster faces.

A GRANDPARENT ASIDE

It's a fact that more and more grandparents are the primary caregivers for their grandchildren. This might be a permanent situation or a temporary one—perhaps just for the summer. If you don't fall into this category, chances are that you know someone who does. If that's the case, be alert for opportunities to have get-togethers with them and their grandchildren. Getting together for coffee (and playtime for the kids) is a simple way to ease the stress that can come with a second round of child rearing. This would be a great learning opportunity for everybody. Swapping parenting duties for a few hours can also provide some relief, time-wise, for care-giving grandparents.

WHILE YOU'RE OUT AT NIGHT:

► Talk about some of the ways people got around in the dark before flashlights existed. (Examples: Candles and candle-holders, lanterns, torches)

► What is the current phase of the moon? Go out the following evening and see if your grandchildren notice if the moon is more or less bright.

► Ask your grandchildren if they can name any animals that do their hunting at night. (Owls, some kinds of snakes, mountain lions.)

► What are the advantages of keen night vision? (Keen night vision helps predators find prey at night and helps nocturnal animals move around in the dark)

► See how many different kinds of light they can list. (Firelight, moonlight, sunlight, light from glow-in-the-dark toys, reflected light, candlelight)

F
L
A
S
H
L
I
G
H
T
S

CONSTELLATIONS

Fun Fact

There are records considering Orion as a constellation as far back as 4000 BC.

Before heading outside to stargaze, spend a bit of time researching the basic constellations. Try a Google search, or better yet, borrow a book from the library. Constellations are groups of stars that can be thought of as connect-the dot patterns. For example, if you connect the dots on the Big Dipper and the Little Dipper, you'd see a big ladle and a smaller ladle. The end of the bowl in the Big Dipper points at the North Star, which always lies north, a handy fact if you've lost your compass and are lost in the woods at night. Sometimes, constellations are talked about in movies. In *Men In Black,* the constellation of Orion is talked about, as "in the belt of Orion." The constellation is often pictured as a hunter, and three bright stars comprise the hunter's belt. The movie plays on this fact. So, knowledge of constellations can not only improve your grandchildren's survival skills, it can improve their appreciation of showings on the silver screen. The nighttime sky is always there, if occasionally obscured by clouds. So this knowledge is something that can be enjoyed on a daily basis. And think about it—if you teach them about constellations, they'll think about you and remember you whenever they spot a constellation.

GRANDPARENT ASIDE

Because we grandparents have already gone through the entire parenting process once, we sometimes enjoy our spare time and don't want to spend all of our retirement with small toddlers or pre-teens. That's more than okay. Don't make the mistake of feeling guilty about it. If you are just on the other side of town from your grandkids, inevitably there will be a weekend when you want to relax and spend in doing whatever you like—solely in the company of adults. Don't feel guilty about this. It's your right. Also be careful about overcompensating for your absence by purchasing extravagant gifts. The gift of your presence is enough.

WHILE YOU'RE FINDING CONSTELLATIONS:

▶ Talk about the position of the constellations in the sky. Do they move around? Why? (The earth rotates on its axis and revolves around the sun, so constellations appear in different regions of the sky and at different times.)

▶ Have your grandchildren point at the North Star, and then lower their arms straight down toward the horizon. Tell them that they are now pointing north!

▶ Ask if they know their birthdays and zodiac signs. Investigate which constellation is associated with their signs. Can you find them in the sky?

TELESCOPE

Fun Fact

The word telescope comes from the Greek tele, meaning "far," and skopein, meaning "to look at."

The next step up from outdoor stargazing is investigation through a telescope. We remember when we first looked at the moon through telescopes. It was astonishing to see shadows on the moon, cast by mountain ranges blocking sunlight, the shadows draped across numerous craters. And the craters were huge! Telescopes have decreased in price thanks to low-cost imports, so see if you can find a deal on one somewhere. If not, a good pair of binoculars will work as well.

As your grandchildren grow, their worlds are constantly expanding. Help to expand their understanding of the world—and the universe in which they live—by introducing them to the hugeness of space. Watch their faces when they realize that the ground on which they stand belongs to a planet that would seem as small as the moon when viewed through a distant telescope. This will help them to understand that objects that seem distant and small can actually be very large. It's all a matter of perspective.

A GRANDPARENT ASIDE

Make sure to occasionally ask to see your grandchildren's school reports. It's important to note that by doing this you are not undermining the authority of the parents, but making sure you have a chance for some input—directly to the kids themselves. Report card time is a great opportunity to talk about how school was when you were the age of your grandchildren. For example, we always walked a mile to school from grade 6 on, often alone. This is a good opportunity also to see the subjects your grandchildren are interested in. This information might be useful later when deciding on a field of study.

WHILE YOU'RE MOON GAZING:

▶ Can your grandkids see the "man in the moon?" Give them a hint; the eyes are formed by craters. Find an image online if you're not sure what to look for.

▶ Sit down and discuss the history of the space exploration program. Try beginning by talking about the Apollo missions and what wonderful technological and scientific feats those missions were—resulting in astronauts walking around on the surface of the moon!

▶ What other planets in our solar system have moons? (All but Mercury and Venus)

▶ Is the moon lifeless? Why? (Having an atmosphere is vital to life)

▶ What's a Moon Pie? Why's it called that? (Moon Pie is actually a brand name for a marshmallow sandwich. The name allegedly comes from the desire of a food maker to develop a snack as big and as round as the moon.)

SHOOTING STARS

Fun Fact

A shooting star is caused by tiny bits of dust and rock or ice falling into the Earth's atmosphere and burning up.

Whenever we pick up the grandkids and arrive at our home late at night, we pause outside before going in and watch for shooting stars. While it's a rare sight, the payoff is great when they finally get to see one. The anticipation is delicious. This bonding activity will have your grandchildren thinking about you every time they see a shooting star, or look for one in the future. If you want to increase your odds of seeing a shooting star, find out when there will be a meteor shower. The American Meteor Society's website, www.amsmeteors.org, has a list of annual meteor showers. The Perseid shower in early August is a popular one.

A GRANDPARENT ASIDE

If you find yourselves in a pinch for time, remember that you can barter or trade time or chores with neighbors or good friends. Just make sure the parents are comfortable with the idea. Some trades include offering to type up a neighboring student's term paper if he teaches your grandchild how to ride a bike. Don't know how to play a musical instrument, but are good at math? Offer a swap of lessons. You could offer to provide a ride to a local soccer game or team practice in exchange for chores around the house, like having your lawn mowed. Use your imagination. This is a situation where working together can provide great benefits for all!

WHILE YOU'RE WATCHING
FOR SHOOTING STARS:

▶ Explain how rocks burn up in the atmosphere because of the heat generated by the friction with the air as they "shoot" through the air.

▶ See if they can imagine what people from thousands of years ago might have thought about shooting stars, before there was a scientific understanding of them.

▶ What do shooting stars do to the moon? (Because it has no atmosphere, they don't burn up—instead, they strike the lunar surface resulting in craters.)

▶ See if they can explain why some movie actors are referred to as shooting stars. (They have very bright but very short careers.)

MUSIC

Fun Fact

Cows usually give more milk
while listening to music.

Amaze your grandchildren by the many ways you can make musical instruments out of household items. Our favorites include making a xylophone out of water glasses by filling them with different levels of water and setting them in a row on a sturdy counter. A reminder for those with young children: tap gently, preferably with something plastic! Broken glass and water over the floor is a bad thing. Try these ideas:

- ▶ String rubber bands across a coffee can or shoe box for a crude guitar.
- ▶ Use a washboard and brush to make a raspy, melodic sound.
- ▶ An oatmeal box can serve as a drum.
- ▶ Simple clapping of hands can provide a background beat.
- ▶ How about a washbasin bass guitar, or just whistling a tune?

You can look online for more ideas. After you and your grandchildren have decided on which musical instrument to play, gather together and play a song. Practice and then provide a live band performance for the parents or other family members. This is something you can encourage your grandchildren to try with their friends for long-lasting fun!

A GRANDPARENT ASIDE

While children have different eating habits, we don't recommend catering to them by preparing three different meals for three children. On the other hand, it's not advisable to try to force food on them that they don't like. Gavin at 7 has a grand total of a dozen foods he'll eat, and refuses new items with great suspicion. The foods he does like are for the most part healthy ones, so we don't push him on it. On the other hand, Kenna loves to try new things (of course, she teethed on beef jerky—not that we recommend this). One day we asked her what was the grossest thing she ate, and she snuggled close and said in a high stage whisper, "When everyone leaves the house, me and Nana eat stinky cheese on toast!"

WHILE YOU'RE MAKING MUSICAL INSTRUMENTS:

▶ Talk about the difference between percussion instruments and wind instruments. (Wind instruments use the flow of air while percussion instruments use the vibration of surfaces in the air.)

▶ Ask if they've ever thought about being professional musicians. Have they ever seen an orchestra on TV?

▶ See how many instruments your grandchildren can name. Don't forget the harmonica! How about the harp?

▶ Ask if they have ever seen a musical. Maybe you can rent *The Music Man* (with its 76 trombones!) or *Mary Poppins* from your local video rental store.

COOKING

Fun Fact

The White House kitchen has five full-time chefs and is able to serve as many as 140 dinner guests.

It seems to us that families used to spend much more of their time in kitchens. Kitchens appear to no longer be the hubs of family activity, perhaps in part because of television. But you can do your part to help turn this around. (Just make sure that if you have a TV in the kitchen, it's turned off.)

There are many ways to have fun in the kitchen. There are different recipes to try, different cooking methods to try, and different spices to try. The point of all of this isn't necessarily just to have fun (although that is certainly part of this), but instead it's to bond with your grandchildren, to talk with them, to share your time. Having kitchen fun is just one of the many ways in this book to strengthen the bonding. It's amazing how often conversations develop when you are in the kitchen with your grandchildren, cooking and preparing meals or having fun making desserts. Here are just a few of the simple things you can do to have kitchen fun:

- Get food dye and mashed potatoes. Make some food dye art, then eat it!
- Try spelling out words with an alphabet cereal or noodle soup (then eat them, of course).
- Use food dye on dry macaroni; get some glue and a backboard, then make a mosaic.
- And of course, there's always the baking soda and vinegar volcano. (Pour them into a volcano-like heap of mashed potatoes for added realism.) If you have a camera, be sure to capture the moment with a picture!

A GRANDPARENT ASIDE

We're sure many of you were taught to "finish your plate—there are staving children in Africa!—or else you can't leave the table." Instead of making them finish the plate, try giving smaller portions. Don't force the issue if they don't want to finish it. Child obesity is rising at a frightening rate, and doctors are seeing juvenile diabetes at near-epidemic rates—and there are even reports of hypertension and heart disease in overweight children. If you can't bear to throw the remaining part of dinner out, cover the plate and stick it in the fridge for later.

WHILE YOU'RE HAVING FUN IN THE KITCHEN:

- Ask them to pick out three food items and read the ingredients to you. This might spark a lot of questions about ingredients that you might not be able to answer. Have your grandchildren find the answers and report back to you.
- Talk about the importance of washing hands when handling food. Have they ever seen news broadcasts that talk about

disease outbreaks that were due to unsanitary food handling at a restaurant?

▶ Talk about some of your memories from kitchens when you were a child. What's different about the kitchens of today?

▶ Have your grandchildren prepare a meal, even if it's just macaroni and cheese with a salad.

C
O
O
K
I
N
G

BIRDFEEDER

Building a birdfeeder can be an excellent way to teach your grandchildren some basics on using tools, such as a hammer. There are many basic designs online, and most local hobby and craft stores carry the basic kits. (All it really takes, though, is a bowl or plate on which to place bird seed.) But it's fun to build something a bit more extravagant—one with wood pegs so the birds can sit.

One idea for a do-it-yourself birdfeeder: take a cardboard milk container, wash it, then fill it halfway with birdseed. Melt shortening over the stove, and when it's ready, pour it into the milk container. Wait for it to cool down. Cut notches in the corners near the bottom, exposing the bird seed. Punch in 2 holes on the sides near the top and tie the ends of a string to these holes. Now, take it outside and loop the string over a strong branch.

You can paint and otherwise decorate your birdfeeder. How about painting on a name, such as *Bob's Diner*? After you've made a birdfeeder, it's time to find a place for it. We suggest someplace up high enough to avoid the cat on the prowl. As always, make sure that you stress the importance of safety when using tools.

1. Wash cardboard milk carton, open top.
2. Fill ½ full with birdseed.
3. Melt shortening, pour over seed and cool.
4. Tie string through holes in top.
5. Cut holes in bottom corners.
6. Hang from tree branch.

A GRANDPARENT ASIDE

We were all told when we were young not to play with our food—well, we're telling you right now—PLAY WITH YOUR FOOD! Kids will enjoy their meals more if they are entertaining to the eyes as well as to the mouth. Try using a cookie cutter to make fun sandwiches, peeling a smiley face into that apple, or drawing a Superman insignia with the ketchup. Cutting a sandwich into 4 strips instead of 4 squares may be all it takes to whet the appetite of that picky toddler.

WHILE YOU'RE MAKING A BIRDFEEDER:

▶ Talk about how seeds eaten by birds are an important method of the cycle of life. (Birds spread the seeds of trees, which take root and become trees themselves.)

▶ See if your grandchildren can describe the beaks of birds that eat seeds as opposed to the beaks of birds (like hawks) that prey on small animals such as rodents. (Seed eaters have vise-like beaks that can break seeds, while meat-eating birds have sharp, curved beaks that can tear apart prey.)

▶ See how many birds you can identify that come to your feeder. Count them every time your grandchildren come over. See if "the word" is spreading among the birds on where to find food.

▶ Do your grandchildren know why rice is no longer suggested be thrown at weddings? (The rice can expand in a bird's stomach and rupture it.)

RECYCLING

Fun Fact

Adults spend an average of 16 times as many hours per year shopping for clothes as they do on planning their retirement.

Before you toss away anything into the trash, take your grandchildren aside and talk about some of the things you are getting ready to throw into the trash. Is there anything that can be done with it? You can go as far as you want with this:

- Take an empty spool of thread and transform it into a pen holder
- Turn a broken bicycle wheel into a base for the growth of vines in your yard
- Drill holes in the sides of an empty plastic coffee can, tie on thin ropes, and you've got a hanging planter
- Food items such as eggshells can be thrown into a compost pile
- Tape a drawing around a soup can and you have a pencil holder

▶ Cut the top third off a cereal box, decorate, and you have a handy magazine holder

Of course, paint and permanent markers can be used to decorate your newly created items. Use your imagination! Better yet, get your grandchildren to use theirs, and you'll end up having hours and hours of bonding fun.

A GRANDPARENT ASIDE

Remember that simple things can fascinate a young child. If you're baking something, turn on the oven light and pull up a chair—you'll be amazed at a 3-year-old's wonder at rising biscuits. Allowing a child to carefully, briefly place a hand high over a heating toaster can be a good way to teach burn safety. It's a good lesson to learn to be cautious where you put your hands, especially in the kitchen. The same goes for cooking on the stovetop—be careful of that sizzling bacon!

WHILE YOU'RE MAKING USEFUL ITEMS:

▶ Talk about landfills and dumps. Landfills might not use trash directly to make useful items, but compared with the old way of dumps being unusable, it's a big improvement! (Landfills are divided into areas in which specific types of items are disposed, such as appliances in one area, building material in another. Grass clippings and leaves go to another area for compost. In the past, dumps were areas in which everything, no matter what, was just . . . well, *dumped,* which could create toxic waste zones.)

- ▶ Ask if your grandchildren know what the following phrase means: One man's trash is another man's treasure. (Some people desire items that other people don't want at all.)
- ▶ Are car tires ever recycled? (Yes; the material is cut up and used to make floor mats, rubberized sidewalks, traffic cones, wheel chocks, road filler, and many other objects.)
- ▶ See if your grandchildren will investigate how nature recycles and report back to you on their next visit.

R
E
C
Y
C
L
I
N
G

4

THE EXTENDED VISIT

▼

MANY GRANDPARENTS TODAY are the primary caregivers for their grandchildren and will find the activities in this chapter invaluable. Even if you're not a daily caregiver, you might find yourself with your grandchildren for an extended stay. Having your grandchildren over for more than an overnight visit provides you with opportunities to begin long-term projects. It also allows you to introduce the grandchildren to your world, your daily habits, and the way you live your life. With these extra opportunities, though, comes the potential for problems. As you probably are well aware from your parenting activities years ago, raising children/grandchildren is a time-intensive endeavor. In the 1960s and 70s, when we were growing up, parental oversight wasn't as necessary. We couldn't go anywhere in the neighborhood without every mom on the block knowing what we were up to! Times have changed drastically. Guiding your grandchildren, interacting with them, doing activities with them while having increasingly deep conversations is a great way to help your grandchildren grow up into successful, moral, responsible adults. And it will give them fond memories for the rest of their lives.

DID YOU KNOW?

Maybe it's because of television, but parents coming from the baby boomer generation seem to spend less time than their parents did talking to their kids about careers and occupations. Use your time with your grandchildren to talk about the various options open to them for careers. Schools these days seem preoccupied with test scores so as not to fall behind, and they seem to be less attentive to helping children think about future careers. There are many more options open to high school students today than in years past. While it's okay to go to college without having decided on an occupation, it would be nice to know your grandkids have at least thought through the possibilities.

So, talk about career paths with your grandchildren. What are the jobs you've had, your friends have had, and maybe some of their aunts and uncles. It's a golden opportunity when you have the grandkids over for an entire week, because you won't feel pressured to get all of the information out in one evening, or one conversation. Have it be an ongoing conversation. Let them think about what was said the night before and come back with questions the following night.

MORE INFORMATION: BOOKS

Carson, Lillian. *The Essential Grandparent: A Guide to Making a Difference.* HCI. Deerfield Beach, Florida: 1997.
In addition to stressing the difference that grandparents can make in their grandchildren's lives, includes helpful ways to improve communication.

Faber, Adele, and Elaine Mazlish. *How to Talk So Kids Will Listen & Listen So Kids Will Talk*. Piccadilly Press. London: 1999.
A helpful book that provides examples of how to talk to children and listen to what they have to say. Helps parents and grandparents to get kids to open up.

More Information: Websites

www.talkingwithkids.org
A website with help on how to talk to children about tough issues like sex, drugs, STDs, and alcohol.
www.neahin.org/canwetalk/resources/parents/index.htm
Provides links to website designed to help with child development.
www.bls.gov/k12
Exploring career information from the Bureau of Labor Statistics, options based on a child's likes and dislikes.
www.kids.gov/k_careers.htm
An excellent website devoted to helping children explore different careers and the resulting different kinds of lives.

CANOEING

Fun Fact

Canoeing was a demonstration sport at the 1924 Paris Olympics. There were six events, and the United States and Canada won all of them.

Canoeing is a great activity that provides exercise as well as the opportunities for long conversations. There are many places that offer canoe rentals. Some will arrange a caravan to drive you upriver so that you will end at your car. Lakes offer more canoeing opportunities, although you won't have the benefit of a current to carry you along. Still, you'll be able to paddle along the shore and maybe see some of nature close up. Remember, if you bring along food and drink, place them in containers that will float. We've found that large zippered bags are essential for water activities like these. It's important to stress safety when you are participating in water activities. Safety vests or other approved flotation devices should always be worn.

A GRANDPARENTING ASIDE

The time you have with your grandchildren is precious. So many of our friends have told us that they wish they had told their grandchildren about this or that. Make the most of your time together and tell them stories about your lives, about what it was like for you when you were their age. What about your parents, and the parents of your parents? Family stories and tales about past generations can so easily get lost, and probably will at some point, but let's not hasten that process! Telling your grandchildren about your history, their history, will give them a sense of their roots, and it will help them to understand who they are and why they came to be like that. For instance, Robin's mother was born blind. A game her mother taught her when she was little was learning how to "see" in the dark. She's now the go-to person whenever there's a power outage.

WHILE YOU'RE CANOEING:

▶ How did Native Americans make their canoes? (They would use fire and sharp stones to hollow out logs to make their canoes or fashion them out of birch bark.)

▶ Demonstrate how a paddle can be used as a rudder when dragged behind the canoe, or as a brake when pushed forward into the water beside the canoe.

▶ Sing a song with a simple but strong beat to coordinate your paddling strokes such as *Row, Row, Row Your Boat.* Maybe call out a cadence—stroke, stroke, stroke!

▶ Ask them to explain the metaphor "Don't rock the boat!"

HOME MOVIES

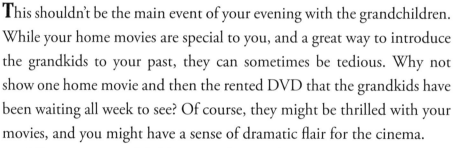

Fun Fact

In 1965 a new movie format called Super 8 was launched, cheaper than other formats and easy to use. It made home movie technology available to the average family, allowing them to film home movies.

This shouldn't be the main event of your evening with the grandchildren. While your home movies are special to you, and a great way to introduce the grandkids to your past, they can sometimes be tedious. Why not show one home movie and then the rented DVD that the grandkids have been waiting all week to see? Of course, they might be thrilled with your movies, and you might have a sense of dramatic flair for the cinema.

When your grandchildren watch your home movies, you can tell them who the people are. It's always fun to see Grandma and Grandpa in their heyday and their parent as a child. "We didn't know you were young once!" they might say. (We've actually heard this one.) It'll be fun and educational, and make sure you talk about it with them after you've watched it.

A GRANDPARENT ASIDE

Sometimes we forget how distracting (and disrupting!) young children can be. There no doubt will come a time when your patience is at an end. While we're not against disciplining children and grandchildren, sometimes it's better if we use our years (and sometimes years and years) of experience to outsmart them. One trick we've used while shopping with an unruly toddler is stopping by the hardware store and picking out a half-dozen paint sample strips. For every five minutes the toddler behaves, they get to hold one color strip. This fascinated them and gave us a half hour of peaceful shopping.

WHILE YOU'RE WATCHING HOME MOVIES:

▶ Would your grandchildren like to make their own movie? What would it be about?

▶ Make them repeat the names of the relatives they saw in the movies. Saying them aloud will help them remember.

▶ Talk about some of the old movies that you remember seeing when you were young.

▶ If your grandchildren are old enough to be computer savvy, ask them to help you preserve your old home movies by converting them to DVDs.

LAKE

We both grew up near the Great Lakes, so for us to consider a body of water a lake, we shouldn't be able to see the far shore. Anything smaller is a pond. We've since adjusted to North Carolina standards, but for this activity, you should visit a large body of water. These are usually geographically significant, so much so that they are discussed in school and on the local newscasts. Your grandkids will remember the trip and think of you at the same time.

When you visit the ocean or a big lake, there's lots to do, from swimming, fishing, looking for seashells, to just exploring. Bring along a camera to capture those memories—or pick up some disposable waterproof ones. Even if you don't go swimming, make sure everyone at least dips a toe into the water. This is for bragging rights! I once had my children put their toes into four of the five Great Lakes during one vacation trip. (We missed Lake Ontario.) A future goal is to reach all five lakes with our grandchildren.

A GRANDPARENTING ASIDE

Although we'd love to make our grandchildren happy all of the time, it's simply not possible. Life doesn't work like that. Steel gets its strength after being subjected to intense heat, and it's a common claim that life's hardships build character. Who hasn't heard the phrase "That which does not kill me makes me stronger?" So, while we all want to protect our grandchildren from difficult times, remember that not only is it impossible to protect them from the bad times, those difficulties may help them grow a quiet, inner strength, and establish a foundation for future self-reliance.

WHILE YOU'RE AT AN OCEAN OR BIG LAKE:

▶ Talk about any experiences you might've had with oceans or big lakes.

▶ How many bodies of water can they name, such as the Pacific and Atlantic Oceans? Don't forget the rivers, such as the Mighty Mississippi.

▶ Can they spell Mississippi?

▶ What careers involve bodies of water? (ecologist, fishermen, search and rescue, the Coast Guard, marine biologists)

▶ What is an ecosystem? (The Chesapeake Bay is a good example; the entire ecological system relies on the codependence of the species that reside there.)

CHORES

It's amazing how soon after graduating high school that children get credit card offers! The last time we checked, there were no school courses to teach kids how to balance a checkbook, or stay out of debt. You can make a significant contribution here. Sit down with them and discuss the basics of finance. Offer to hire them to do chores, such as weeding or mowing the yard. You should agree to the payment in advance. Tell your grandchildren that you'd like to have them save the money for something, and offer to keep the money in your house, or have the parents set up a savings account. It's a great way to get the grandkids saving money for something they want to get. If your grandchildren are industrious, they might start coming to you asking for more jobs, or offering their services to the neighbors! Here are some possible jobs and chores:

- ▶ Organizing photographs, bookshelves or recipes
- ▶ Making personalized stationery on your computer
- ▶ Helping clean and organize attics and basements

- Tutoring in computer skills
- Watering plants
- Washing windows
- Shoveling snow
- Raking leaves
- Walking or taking care of pets
- Wrapping gifts
- Washing cars

Remember, the object here isn't for them to have fun (although they very well might), but to do a job for you and to get paid doing it. You might not want them to pick the chore.

A GRANDPARENTING ASIDE

We believe it's very important to try *not* to pass along your own fears and phobias. If you're afraid of spiders, saying "Would you please get rid of that THING?" is much more acceptable than screeching and running. Likewise for other fears such as a fear of heights or claustrophobia. The same goes for foods. If you don't like a particular food, stay neutral on the subject. Make a game out of it by saying "Euwww, I can't believe you ate that! You're so brave!" Sometimes we like to feel better about ourselves by getting everyone to understand our fears, maybe even to the point of sharing them. Resist! Let your grandkids explore their worlds without preconceived fears and phobias.

While you're assigning chores:

- Financial planner Laura Hinton recommends children have three allowance jars—one for spending, one for saving, and one for giving. Suggest this to their parents.

▶ Talk about some of the jobs a handyman might perform. Have you ever hired one? What for?

▶ Talk about some of the odd jobs you did in your youth.

▶ Calculate how much your grandchildren earned per hour after the job is completed.

▶ What are some of the differences between an hourly rate and a flat rate?

MOVIES

While you can also do this during an overnight visit, it does take up a lot of time where you are not directly engaged with your grandkids. That's why this activity is better for an extended visit. It's time spent together doing something enjoyable. What grandchild wouldn't be tickled seeing the latest available animated Disney movie with Grandma and Grandpa? More and more of these movies are being created to be enjoyed by adults. Watching a movie together will give them something to look forward to when they come over. Let them give you their movie suggestions, but make sure they aren't selecting titles their parents have objected to. Consider purchasing their favorites. Many rental stores sell used DVDs and video cassettes. Start a list and have your grandchildren update it periodically.

A GRANDPARENT ASIDE

It's common to warn children and grandchildren about talking to strangers, but a sobering fact is that 30 to 40% of abuse is done by a family member, and another 50% is by someone who is trusted and known by the family. Did you know that only 35% of sexual abuse is ever reported? While we don't want to worry you, it never hurts to be more aware of who is in contact with your grandchildren. Stay alert. Talk to your grandchildren about what they do and who they interact with. Listen to your instincts about things that sound out of place. Make sure your grandchildren know how to call 911. Explain how some abductors will entice children with games that sound like loads of fun, and perhaps candy, too! Talk about some of the things that they might say in order to frighten a child into not talking about some incident, such as threatening to hurt a sibling, but insist that telling a parent or grandparent is always the right decision.

WHILE YOU'RE WATCHING MOVIES:

▶ Talk about some of the movies you watched when you were younger. Did you see a Ronald Reagan movie? Do your grandchildren recognize the name?

▶ What are your grandchildren's favorite movies? What specifically did they like about it? How about their least favorite?

▶ Imagine yourselves as movie critics writing local columns for a newspaper.

▶ Name the three best parts of the movie.

▶ Would there be anything different if they had been directing the movie?

▶ If there were special effects, go over those parts. It's important they understand the difference between reality and what they see on the theater screen.

SWIMMING

Swimming can provide great exercise. Of course, younger children must be supervised when they are in the water. We believe that children should learn how to swim when they are very young. Check your local YMCAs for classes, or ask friends and neighbors for a referral. It seems every year there is another story of a drowning that took place when a parent's attention was diverted for a short time. Familiarity with water and strong swimming skills will go a long way to helping children play safely in water. We suggest playing water games to help your grandkids become more comfortable in the water. Try the game of shark, which is basically a game of tag. The grandparent is the "shark" and runs through the water try to gobble up the grandkids. No fair getting out of the water! Try to sneak up on them by using other people in the water as shields. When a grandchild is "gobbled up," that child becomes a shark, too. The last grandchild to be gobbled up is the winner and gets to be the first shark for the next round.

A GRANDPARENT ASIDE

When you find yourself sitting with your grandchild in a public area, perhaps waiting in a doctor's office or having a snack in the local mall's food court, do some "people watching." What are the differences you see in people? (The way they dress, walk, and talk; their mannerisms and hairstyles.) This helps your grandchildren learn about diversity. Everybody is different if you look close enough! It also helps your grandchildren to learn to be observant. Let them know it's not nice to make fun of people for the way they dress, talk, walk, and look. Ask your grandkids if they think the people's feelings would be hurt if they overheard your comments. If there aren't many people wandering by, count the ways that you are the same as your grandchildren. Do you share family traits? What color are your eyes? Maybe you have narrow feet, just like your grandchildren!

WHILE YOU'RE SWIMMING
AND PLAYING SHARK:

▶ This is a great time for physical "roughhousing." While playing rough in a house can result in broken vases and coffee tables, it's less risky to "throw" a grandchild into a body splash. Our grandchildren love it and always come back for more.

▶ Ask if they've seen the movie *Jaws*. Would they like to?

▶ Do their parents take them swimming or play "shark"?

▶ How many swim strokes they know? Demonstrate the side stroke, back stroke, and the butterfly.

BAKING

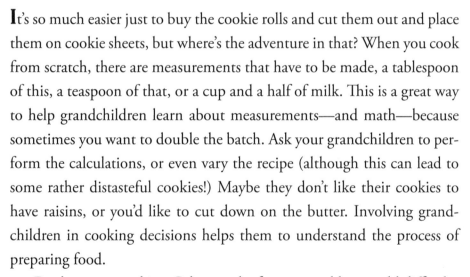

Fun Fact

Chips Ahoy! cookies are baked in ovens that are as long as football fields, and have more than 4,000 cookies coming out of the oven every minute.

It's so much easier just to buy the cookie rolls and cut them out and place them on cookie sheets, but where's the adventure in that? When you cook from scratch, there are measurements that have to be made, a tablespoon of this, a teaspoon of that, or a cup and a half of milk. This is a great way to help grandchildren learn about measurements—and math—because sometimes you want to double the batch. Ask your grandchildren to perform the calculations, or even vary the recipe (although this can lead to some rather distasteful cookies!) Maybe they don't like their cookies to have raisins, or you'd like to cut down on the butter. Involving grandchildren in cooking decisions helps them to understand the process of preparing food.

Don't stop at cookies. Cakes can be fun too, and layers add difficulty for older grandkids. How about cupcakes? If there's a birthday coming up, a graduation, or another special day, baking could be a perfect gift. Don't forget that you can add special holiday decorations to your cakes and cookies. Use sprinkles and icing tubes, or some colored frosting, put in a Zip-Loc bag, snip a corner, and use it to write on the cookies or cake.

A GRANDPARENT ASIDE

If your grandchildren's parents are divorced or are getting divorced (and 50% of people nowadays are), talk to your grandkids about the process. You should be neutral in tone, no matter what you think about the circumstances. The grandchildren will still have two parents. How do your grandchildren feel about it? Tell them that you worry about them, and that you know everything will be okay, but that it's a grandparent's prerogative to worry. This will open lines of communication, and it'll let the child know that it's okay to feel differently than the adults. For example, you can let them know that you understand why children might not like some house rules, but that you might feel differently. Make sure to tell them that only grown-up married people get divorced—many children feel threatened that a parent will want to be divorced from the children, too.

WHILE YOU'RE MAKING COOKIES OR BAKING CAKES:

▶ What were some of the meals prepared by your parents (the children's great-grandparents)?

▶ Was your milk delivered to your doorstep?

▶ What are their favorite kinds of cookies and cake?

▶ What kinds of cakes are made at the store?

▶ Do elves really make cookies?

▶ Talk about the expression, "you can't have your cake and eat it, too." What does it mean?

GROCERIES

We aren't gourmet diners, but when we took our grandchildren to an upscale food market, they were amazed. It was as though they'd never seen such a variety of food, and mostly what they'd seen in supermarkets were boxes and cans of food, not the food itself. We pointed out some of the gourmet coffee beans and the exotic fruit and vegetables. There was also a wide array of hand-made pasta. Make a list of the foods that you might like to splurge on one day, and take your grandchildren to a gourmet market, a vegetable market, or a farmer's market. Allow them to pick out one special item that you'll buy for them. (Our grandkids picked out nectarines.) Why not set them to a task, such as finding the linguini? And as a bonus when you get home, you get to prepare a very nice meal and share it with your grandchildren.

A GRANDPARENT ASIDE

Talk careers once in a while with your grandchildren, using family members as examples. "Uncle Bill is a mechanic—he repairs cars that are broken. Aunt Kathy's a nurse. She helps sick people get better. Cousin Ed is a teacher." One of our sons, when he was very, very young, wanted to be a garbage truck driver. He thought they got to keep everything they picked up! This was the same child who thought a tomato and a tornado were the same things, which resulted in a terrified child during storm warnings. He was picturing a huge red fruit spinning its way toward him, ready to fall from the sky and squash him. He turned out okay, although he still refuses to eat tomatoes. In any case, it's great to get your grandchildren to think about all of the different careers that are out there. Your grandchildren might want to learn more about the careers you mention, so be prepared to make telephone calls to the family member and let your grandchildren find out more directly from the source.

WHILE YOU'RE GROCERY SHOPPING:

▶ Talk about all of the different foods that come from corn. (Cans of corn. Corn on the cob. Creamed corn. Cornbread. Tortillas. Corn oil. And that's not even mentioning ethanol!)

▶ What is a "herbivore"? (an animal that eats plants to live) A "carnivore"? (an animal that eats meat to live) One that eats both? (an omnivore) What grocery sections would each dine in?

▶ Can they name different cuts of beef? Head over to the meat counter and see if they can tell the difference between them.

▶ Go over to the cheese section and see how many kinds of cheese there are. What makes them different?

SOCK PUPPETS

Sock puppets are easy to make. Purchase white socks and put your hand in one, keeping your fingers locked straight and your thumb stiff. Stuff some of the sock between the thumb and index finger. This is the puppet's mouth. Use a marker to highlight it, add eyes and a nose above, and you're ready to go! You can add other features like hats, ties, or scarves by drawing them on or by pinning on a small circle of cloth. Have fun with this and let your grandchildren's imagination run wild. Then, discuss the creation of a sock puppet play. What kind of characters do they want? (Hint: a classroom setting is good as they will be familiar with it.) Assign some parts and come up with a storyline. Will your play be about a classroom bully who gets his comeuppance, or a school kid who wins a contest and gets to ride on a NASA shuttle and orbit Earth? Maybe it's about how two friends make up after a disagreement (and shake hands!) If they are comfortable with presenting it before an audience, practice and perform it for the other family members.

A GRANDPARENT ASIDE

Children, especially active ones, have different water requirements than adults and will get dehydrated more quickly. Make sure your grandchildren have plenty of water available. Children also tend to get into "food ruts," when they favor certain foods and refuse to try different ones. It's a good idea to go over a food chart with your grandchildren. Glue magazine photos of the different food groups onto a standard sheet of paper and keep it on your refrigerator with a magnet. Good eating habits are developed early in children, and they will be habits they will have for the rest of their lives. There *is* a national obesity epidemic. Remind your grandkids that there is a difference between eating food for health and eating food out of habit. Talk about how some people are binge eaters—not a healthy lifestyle!

WHILE YOU'RE MAKING SOCK PUPPETS:

▶ Make a joke about feigning that you don't care about something and say, "Tell it to the hand because I'm not listening."

▶ Get them to try out different voices, from deep and raspy to high and squeaky.

▶ Can they remember any famous sayings, such as "Remember the Alamo!" and say them with their sock puppets? If they don't know any, tell them one or look some up online.

▶ Have them sing a song with their sock puppets.

AT THE GRANDKIDS' HOUSE

▼

WHEN YOU ARE visiting your children and grandchildren at their home, remember that this is your adult child's house, so you should abide by their rules. However, this is also the domain of your grandchildren, and they will probably be eager to show you their world. Let them! They might want to show off their rooms, take you on a tour of the house, or point out recent home improvements.

The primary reason for your visit may not be to visit with your grandchildren, but don't forget to give them a little of your time. Don't make the mistake of just communicating with your son or daughter (and their spouse) and ignoring the grandchildren. Take the visit as an opportunity to relate to them in their world. Even if your visit will be very quick, it doesn't take much time to do the first activity in this chapter. We're sure that you can think of more.

DID YOU KNOW?

Nutrition knowledge has expanded quite a bit since we were children. Although obesity can be linked to nutrition, good nutrition is an entire subject by itself. There are, for example, thin children who do not eat the right kinds of food. Some are malnourished. It's important to teach *what* to eat as well as how much. We remember when the advice was to make sure you ate something from each of the five basic food groups. This has been expanded into a food pyramid. The idea was that the groups at the bottom of the pyramid were the foundation for growth, with the higher-up groups building on that foundation, and all for a rock-solid pyramid of human development. Nowadays, the pyramid has been expanded to include many different groups, not just fruits and vegetables and dairy products. Dietary suggestions now include items like nuts and legumes, plant oils (like canola), and whole grain foods. Another group in the pyramid isn't food at all, but rather exercise and weight control. This is an excellent idea, because eating too much of the right foods can still lead to obesity. And exercise is one of the keys to a healthy lifestyle. Check out the government's website (www.nutrition.gov/) for more of the latest dietary suggestions. And if you haven't had the healthiest of eating habits, don't assume that what worked for you will work for your grandchildren. We've heard people say things like they've lived long lives and never paid any attention to nutrition. Fine, but think about your grandchildren and let them know what good, nutritious eating habits are.

MORE INFORMATION: BOOKS

Evers, Connie Liakos. *How to Teach Nutrition to Kids.* 24 Carrot Press. Portland: 2006.
Loaded with ideas to make nutrition education fun and interesting for children. There are also activities and crafts that illustrate the ideas.

Haas, Ellen. *Fit Food: Eating Well For Life.* Hatherleigh Press. New York: 2005.

Identifies 21 fit foods and has over 200 simple recipes for nutritious meals. Also has hints for cooking food so it retains the most nutrients.

MORE INFORMATION: WEBSITES

www.mypyramid.gov

Helps you to personalize meals, using the kinds of foods and the amounts that are right for you while keeping nutrition in mind.

www. nutrition.gov

Provides up-to-date news about nutrition and health topics.

www.usda.gov

Website of the U.S. Department of Agriculture. Has information about regulations and recalls. Includes food and nutrition links.

www.kids.gov/k_health.htm

An excellent website directed at children, answering such questions as why children should wash their hands and what vaccines do.

TOYS AND HOBBIES

Fun Fact

The first electric-powered model trains appeared in the late 1800s.

Depending on the ages of your grandchildren, you'll ask them to ei-ther bring out their favorite toy to show you or demonstrate a hobby to show off. It's your job as a grandparent to be properly awed by the magnificence of their toy, and impressed by the skill with which they play with it. Do you have a stamp collector or an artist in the family? Prompt them to speak up if they are shy. You can also have them show you their schoolwork. Which schoolbooks and papers are they studying? Ask to see them.

A GRANDPARENTING ASIDE

The grandparents seldom dictate the day-to-day lifestyles of their grand-children. Some parents are extremely scheduled, sending their children here or there to do this or that at every minute of every day. At the other end of the spectrum, some parents will allow their kids to do just about anything they want (or at least it seems like that to us). There should be a happy medium that allows both the children and the grandchildren to make scheduling choices. Maybe let the grandchildren decide the menu for evening dinner. Maybe let them decide on where to go on a Sunday drive. Maybe let them decide which clothes they want to wear to go shopping. The point here is to help your children to empower the grandchildren in a way that helps them learn about decision making, and to make sure they understand that they need to live with the consequences of those decisions.

WHILE YOU'RE LOOKING AT THEIR TOYS/HOBBIES:

▶ What are some of the toys you had as a child?

▶ How did kids entertain themselves before the days of 9,000 channels on cable TV?

▶ How many different hobbies can they (and you) think of?

▶ What are the favorite toys and hobbies of their friends?

▶ How many toys do they have? If they don't know, have them count them in front of you. (How many toys does a child really need?)

MULTIPLICATION TABLE

Fun Fact

Albert Einstein, Thomas Edison, Nelson
Rockefeller and General George Patton
all had learning disabilities.

One thing that most people seem pressed for is spare time. So just how do you find the time to help your grandchildren learn and appreciate math? Here's a great suggestion. A lot of car rides are in the five- to thirty-minute range. When you have your grandchildren in the car, go through the multiplication table with them. Remember that? It's a grid with 1 through 9 in the top row and in the first column. So you go row by row, multiplying the column number by the row number. The second row is 2, so 2 times 1 is 2, 2 times 2 is 4, 2 times 3 is 6, and so on. Sounds easy, yes, but when you get to row seven, column six and try to remember what 7 times 6 is, you might be needing your grandchildren for help! This is a great way to help your grandkids to remember the multiplication table, and it takes so little of your time that you can do it repeatedly without getting bogged down in the repetition of it. After a couple of months, your grandkids will be spouting out multiplication facts left and right, and you can smile at their accomplishment because of the role you played!

A GRANDPARENTING ASIDE

Many people are afraid of math. If the subject is addressed early enough in your grandkid's lives, they can escape math phobia. Math is the foundation for many other subjects in the sciences. We suggest bringing up the subject whenever you use math, even for little things. For example, if you're trying to figure out how many seedlings will fit into your garden plot, bring your grandchildren into the discussion. Show them any equations you think are relevant. If you're trying to figure out how much money taxes are going to add to an item's cost at the store, tell your grandchildren how you arrive at the figure. Sometimes we use so much math, we forget we're using it. Make sure to engage your grandchildren in your math processes, and the calculations will pay off when they become adults.

WHILE YOU'RE HELPING WITH MATH:

▶ What numbers do you see in everyday life? (Prices in a supermarket to gas station signs, from phone numbers to digital clocks. Ask your grandchildren to find more and report back to you.)

▶ What math did they learn in school last week? If they can't remember, tell them to pay attention and report back to you next week on what they learned.

▶ How fast can they count to ten, twenty, or one hundred? Gear this towards their age.

▶ Can they count the coins you have lying around? A coin jar would be great! Younger grandchildren can count coin by coin, while older ones can add up the change they can hold in one hand.

FLOOR PLANS

Floor plans are a great way to teach your grandchildren about spatial drawings and representative maps. There are two ways you can do this. The first is a fact-finding mission around the house, requiring a tape measure and careful measurements of each room. You'll acquire some grid paper and decide on a key (such as one grid is 1 foot, so a 10-foot by 10-foot room is shown on the grid as a 10-square by 10-square area). You can get as detailed as your grandchildren want. The second option will be to sketch out the floor plan without taking measurements. Then, you can walk around the house and see how accurate their memory actually was. You can also sketch out the floor plan of the house you grew up in, or plot out the house of your grandkids' dreams. Do they want to live in a castle with a moat?

A GRANDPARENT ASIDE

As your grandchildren approach or enter high school, they are going to be exposed to the many vices of our country's teenage population. We suggest talking with your older grandchildren about alcohol, sex, and drugs (even if you're a former Flower Child and have qualms about being hypocritical). The movie *Reefer Madness,* which was originally shot in 1936 and financed by a church group as a teaching tool for parents, is a great way to broach the subject. While some of you ex-hippies might have actually "inhaled" (unlike Bill Clinton in his famous denial) as teenagers yourself, today's world has crack, crank, crystal meth, ecstasy, and the date-rape drug GHB, and these are no laughing matter. Watch the movie, then talk to your grandchildren about the real risks out there, and don't forget about the dangers of drinking alcohol in excess, drinking and driving, or drinking at all when underage. Another, perhaps larger, problem is the abuse of prescription drugs. There's an erroneous assumption that because these are "prescribed" drugs, they are safe. Wrong! Contact local high schools or D.A.R.E. programs to find out what your area's prevalent prescription drug problems are.

While you're drawing floor plans:

▶ Have everybody tell a story about something (true or false) that happened in a house.

▶ How do plumbing and electricity get connected to a house? (If you're not sure, have your grandkids find out and report back to you.)

▶ Calculate the total square footage of the floor space by multiplying the width and length of each room and adding the results.

▶ Ask them to describe their "dream house."

MORSE CODE

Fun Fact

The last Coast Guard navigation station still using Morse code transmitted its last message on March 31, 1995 from Chesapeake, Virginia.

Morse code was used long before voices could be carried over telephone lines (indeed, before telephone lines existed). It used telegraph lines. Using a series of clicks and pauses (and some time to decipher), you could send any message you wanted. In recent years Morse code has still been in use; submarines lost power, and crew members communicated by banging out Morse code messages on the hull. It will take a bit of time to memorize the code, but you don't need to worry about memorizing it at this point. You can easily find Morse code online or at your local library. Just print it out from your computer or use a copy machine at the library. Then, go into separate rooms and tap out your messages on the walls. Won't it be great when your grandkids go to school and brag about how they communicated messages via Morse code on their last visit with their grandparents?

A GRANDPARENT ASIDE

"Look how much they've grown!" This is almost a grandparent's default greeting after any appreciable amount of time has passed since the last meeting. Sometimes this helps us to realize they are growing up quickly, and we may need to talk to them about some of the dangers in the world around them. We've already mentioned drug and alcohol use; there's another activity that can be addicting: gambling. There's nothing wrong with an occasional friendly bet or buying lottery tickets (for adults), but whether it's because of the lure of quick money or excitement, there are people who grow dependent on gambling, who need to get a "fix" by placing bet after bet. Keep an eye on the youngsters, and when you hear them say, "Wanna bet?" have a talk with them about gambling and how dangerous it can be. Remember that it's best that people only bet with money that they can afford to lose.

WHILE YOU'RE LEARNING MORSE CODE:

▶ What's the signal for SOS? (Dot dot dot. Dash dash dash. Dot dot dot.) This shows up often in film.

▶ Write a message to their parents in Morse code.

▶ Remind them to talk to their teachers about learning more about secret or spy codes.

▶ Get a T-shirt and write their names on it in Morse code.

PETS

Of course, the parents have the final and absolute say about what pets can be brought into their houses. A family pet can be a wonderful way to teach grandchildren responsibility as well as helping them feel more connected and loved. Even the most adamantly anti-pet parents can probably be convinced to let their kid have an ant farm, especially if precautions are taken so the little creatures won't escape. Aquariums are great, too, but they require more care. Aquariums that aren't regularly cleaned can end up sending bad odors throughout the house—not to mention the dead fish! Grandchildren can spend hours watching their industrious ants digging tunnels and building their society. If they're in school, an ant farm can provide material for a school paper. You can suggest that the grandchild take pictures once a week so that progress in the construction of the tunnels can be easily seen in photographs.

A GRANDPARENTING ASIDE

Sometimes we, as grandparents, make great plans for a visit with our grandchildren. We might even spend weeks in preparation. As with everything else in life, sometimes things don't go according to plan. You might have planned for an outing and the weather is bad, or your grandchild's foot is in a cast, or maybe an event you were looking forward to gets cancelled. This is a great opportunity to show your grandchildren, by example, what to do when things don't go right. (Hopefully, the parents are contributing to their maturity in this regard.) Have a Plan B. It's your right to express disappointment that the original plan didn't work, but we're grown-ups now and shouldn't harp on not getting our way. By giving your grandchildren this example, you'll teach them not to stop trying when there are setbacks—and life is filled with them. It's not the number of setbacks that define us—it's how we deal with them.

WHILE YOU'RE TALKING ABOUT PETS:

▶ What kinds of pets did you have as a child?

▶ Discuss how much the care products for pets have improved. (There are dog exercise machines available for overweight canines!)

▶ How do ants store food for the winter? (Recite the fable about how the lazy grasshopper scoffed and ridiculed the ants until the snows came.)

▶ Even if you can't name all of the ants, you could give them a group name. How about Dirt Diggers?

▶ What is the difference between dog years and human years? (1 dog year equals 7 human years of relative growth.)

▶ What kind of pets would your grandchildren like if they lived on a farm?

FAMILY TREE

Fun Fact

Princess Diana was related to Humphrey Bogart; they were seventh cousins.

It's a great idea to sit down to draw a family tree for your grandchildren. Keep it simpler the younger they are; family trees can get very large very quickly and names will blur for younger grandchildren. Things that may seem so obvious to you may need explaining to them. For example, our oldest grandson Gavin, after we made a reference to our daughter, asked in surprise, "You know Aunt Sara?" We had to explain that Sara was our daughter, their father's sister. Remember how inexperienced grandchildren are! Their worlds are very small, and it's one of the great roles that grandparents can play—expanding their universe. They will be amazed to see how many people they are related to, begin to understand their place in the family, and learn how a family branches into the past and the future.

A GRANDPARENT ASIDE

Just because it used to be true doesn't mean it was ever right! For example, Dr. Spock's bestselling book on childcare was first published in

1946. While much of his advice is tried and true, many strides have been made in the raising of children since then. For example, Dr. Spock had originally advocated placing infants on their front sides when it was time to sleep, which later was understood to increase the risk of SIDS (Sudden Infant Death Syndrome). We're sure everyone remembers the old (and unsafe) advice for teething babies: rubbing a drop of whiskey on their gums! Don't assume that because you heard something once, it works—or that it is true.

WHILE YOU'RE DRAWING YOUR FAMILY TREE:

▶ How much of the family tree can your grandchildren remember after you put it away?

▶ What were some quirks of the older generation in your family? (For example, our Uncle Benny played the accordion in his sleep, while we like to keep gator plush toys in the bathroom.)

▶ What are some of the occupations of tree members?

▶ Make sure to explain how last names can change with marriage.

VIDEO GAMES

Fun Fact

Atari's home version of PONG was released for Christmas of 1975, and launched the home video game revolution.

Much has been written about video games, and a lot of it points to the harmful effects (citing obesity figures, for example). While this is true enough for anyone who spends all of their days sitting in front of their TV, playing video games occasionally won't harm anyone. All things in moderation! There's a lot of good that can be taken from video games, such as help with hand-eye coordination from first-person shooters, or intellectual stimulation from strategy games. So, have your video console ready, along with a few games, for those rainy days. Ask your grandchildren what kind of games they would like you to keep on hand. Many of the games for younger kids are designed to be educational, so be sure to check them out even if they aren't some of the grandkids' suggestions. If you live close enough to their house, and they have a game console, you could drive over and borrow it with the parents' permission, of course. Keep all of the grandchildren involved, even if there are only two handsets, by initiating round-robin games, or by sitting out yourself to watch from the sidelines. What about taking five-minute turns? If arguments begin, put the game console away and watch the rain (which, we believe, the grandchildren will agree is much less fun).

A GRANDPARENTING ASIDE

We sometimes think that the children of today are losing their sense of play. Oh, if you go by schoolyards, you'll hear plenty of excited shouts and laughing, but at home they face some plenty serious subjects. Parents can obsess with getting into the right college, getting good grades, or excelling at sports. When was the last time they had a chance to just goof off with their parents or grandparents? How about a good tickling? Or just acting silly and rolling around on the grass? Structured play is fine and good, but unstructured play can be very important. Think about your youth and the times when you laughed uncontrollably with your friends. Aren't those memories a great thing to pass down to your grandchildren? The next time your plans are washed out by rain, act silly by acting horribly distraught (overacting) and saying the world is ending! Roll around on the carpet in fake agony. The grandkids will catch on quickly and laugh and roll around with you.

WHILE YOU'RE PLAYING VIDEO GAMES:

▶ Ask about the video games they have at their house. Which is their favorite? Why?

▶ Describe the games you played in your youth. (Pinball machines, arcade games?)

▶ What kind of video game would they create if they were video game designers?

▶ Remember to act silly!

6

SHORT TRIPS

▼

QUICK—WHAT'S ANOTHER WAY to get away from the TV? Go on a short trip! We can resemble a couch-potato as easily as the next person. It's so tempting just to stay at home when you have those special moments with your grandchildren, and you've been busy all week, but there are so many things to do nearby! When we were active parents, of course, we were even busier.

There are a lot of local activities available that their parents might not have the time or inclination to go to. Every activity that involves getting out of the house helps support a more active lifestyle for both you and your grandchildren. Whether it's a ten- or thirty-minute drive, this is a great way to help your grandchildren expand their horizons and explore the world around them. If you live in a large city, take mass transit. Our grandchildren still haven't traveled on a train—but we're working on it!

DID YOU KNOW?

At some point (probably sooner that you'd like), you're going to be faced with grandchildren who are approaching driving age. More and more teenagers are driving these days. According to the National Highway Traffic Safety Administration, the number of teenagers out on the road has increased by 5 million over the last 10 years. They now make up more than one-fifth of the driving population. Although there are many safety programs designed to help teenagers learn to drive safely, it's always a good idea to go over some of the more important topics with the parents. For example, automobile maintenance is extremely important. Teenagers, as well as everybody else, should know how to check tire pressure. Tires not properly inflated can increase the risk of an accident. They should have a set of jumper cables and know how to use them. While it might be likely that a teenager will have a cell phone to call in case of a flat tire, there are dead zones for cell phones, and it's a good idea to teach teenagers how to change a tire. At a minimum, they should be aware of how to use a flat tire fixer can, because help might not always be available. The car should be equipped with an emergency kit, containing flares, a flashlight, a tire-inflating can, and a first-aid kit. (See below for more information on what to have in a kit.) Remember, it's easy to assume your grandchildren are learning all of this from their driver's education classes, but we all know assumptions can lead us into trouble, and when it comes to auto safety, there's often no room for mistakes.

More Information: Books

Berardelli, Phil. *Safe Young Drivers: A Guide for Parents and Teens.* Nautilus Communications. Vienna, Virginia: 2006.
A complete course for beginning drivers.

Joseph, James. *110 Car and Driving Emergencies and How to Survive Them: The Complete Guide to Staying Safe on the Road.* The Lyons Press. Guilford, Connecticut: 2003.

Quick answers to any problem a driver will possibly face.

Moore, Terry Lynn. *Teaching Your Teen Behind the Wheel: A Parent's Guide for their Teenage Driver.* AuthorHouse. Bloomington, Indiana: 2004.

This book will help teach a new driver to be safer, and to get better results in preparation for driving.

Smith, Timothy C. *Crashproof Your Kids: Make Your Teen a Safer, Smarter Driver.* Fireside. New York, New York: 2006.

Is there anything scarier to a parent than handing over the car keys to a teenager?

MORE INFORMATION: WEBSITES

www.redcross.org/prepare/kit/kit_8_2.asp

A good list from the Red Cross for what to have in a car emergency kit.

www.teendriving.com

An extensive website with a section on tips for a teenager buying a first car and safety topics for teen drivers. Includes safe driving strategies.

autos.msn.com/advice/article.aspx?contentid=4021156

An article that talks about the different safety features of cars and different aspects of safety that can vary with car models.

www.autoextra.com/firstride/do-press

A list of the top 10 student cars and the reasons for their inclusion in the list, including safety and mileage considerations.

FESTIVAL

Local festivals are usually advertised in the local newspapers, on bulletin boards at grocery stores, and on community websites. Parents are usually eager to attend these as well, so tag along, or, even better, go a second time alone with your grandchildren. Ask them to show you all the things they noticed during their first visit. Country fairs are popular in the summer. In the fall, watch for harvest festivals. (These are great for buying pumpkins, if it's near Halloween.) There are many spring festivals, too, celebrating the return of warmer weather, often around the time flowers start to bloom. Many areas have crop-specific festivals, such as strawberry and apple festivals. Make sure to check the "life" or "community" section of your local newspaper. Local news shows often have announcements, too. With any festival, we suggest bringing along some snacks, especially if you know there will be an excessive amount of fast food available. Many of the festivals have nutritious food, too; just be choosy. We're not against the occasional candy apple, but keep it within reason. Too many candy apples, cotton candy, and soda pops are a bad thing. We both admit, though, to fond memories of cotton candy and candy apples at county fairs, so by all means let the grandkids have a taste!

A GRANDPARENTING ASIDE

When your grandchildren are old enough, say, middle school and above, consider watching a national news broadcast with them. (If they're younger, try the Discovery Channel.) We're not suggesting that children would be interested in learning the size of any particular trade imbalance, but a natural disaster that results in thousands of deaths should be something even your young grandchild should know about. Riots, pandemics, wars—all of these are newsworthy, and we would expect our older grandchildren to have some knowledge of them. Sometimes, these events are covered in their classrooms or places of worship. When your grandchildren come over or you visit them, have a talk with them about what's in the news. Sit down and watch a national news broadcast and talk about what you believe is important. This can be a valuable tool for teaching your grandkids good communication skills. It'll help your grandchildren during the week because it'll give them things to talk about with their teachers and peers. Many natural disasters, such as Hurricane Katrina, result in opportunities to volunteer for charity work, which is something else you can discuss with them as a result of watching the news together.

WHILE YOU'RE AT A SEASONAL FESTIVAL:

▶ What were some of the festivals and parades you attended as a child?

▶ How have things changed?

▶ What role does food play in festivals (especially harvest festivals and state fairs)?

▶ Can they explain the changes of seasons to you?

▶ Which season is their favorite? Why?

▶ Which winter do you remember most? Which summer? What about your grandkids?

LOCAL ACTIVITIES

Fun Fact

Newsprint is one of the easiest paper products to recycle because of the ease with which it can be turned back into pulp.

If you live in a large metropolitan area, local can be relative. There's usually a "local" section of the big newspapers. Encourage your grandchildren to look through the community events page and find a local activity they think will be fun. They will be amazed how many clubs and other organizations have meetings and events. Sometimes it's a local fishing exhibition. Sometimes it's a bake-off. Maybe it's a used book sale. There are even yard and garage sales listed. Have your grandkids make a decision to attend one activity. It's fun just to look through the items to see what other people once had thought important enough to buy or make, but remind the kids you don't have to participate in the event to have fun. Maybe the Boy Scouts are having an awards ceremony, or the volunteer firemen are having practice at the station. Another event that we've attended is the opening of a park. That is a great excuse to go to the park later, too. You can also have your grandkids ask their teachers for inspiration. If all else fails, suggest a trip to a community pool or the nearest theme park.

A GRANDPARENTING ASIDE

It seems to us that most parents want to do a good job, and they will often look for advice. When they come to you, make sure that the advice you give is practical. While it's great advice to open up the lines of communication, this isn't useful without the accompanying advice of HOW. Try giving the parents the conversation starters and activities that loosen up the grandchildren (so that they don't feel like they are being grilled for information) that you'll find in these pages. Anyone can give great advice. Give them yours, and make sure it's practical.

WHILE YOU'RE HAVING LOCAL FUN:

▶ How have newspapers changed through the years?

▶ How have they stayed the same?

▶ Can they describe what a "community" is?

▶ How large or small can a community be?

▶ What is a "neighborhood watch?"

PARADES

Parades are usually listed in the newspaper and are often announced on local news broadcasts. Even in our small town, there are several parades each year, and nearly everybody is either in the parade or watching it. (We're still trying to figure out why the rear of the parade consists of people in cars with nothing special about them other than being highly polished.) But we live near larger cities, too, and attend the larger parades in those. Everybody's tastes vary, but we enjoy marching bands because we like live musical performances. Parades can be a great way to introduce youngsters to music and how many different instruments can come together to produce toe-tapping songs. In addition to parades on holidays such as the Fourth of July and Memorial Day, there are often parades near the end of the football season for bowl games. We suggest bringing a camera so you can take pictures, print them, and go over them with your grandchildren while talking about the fun time you had.

A GRANDPARENT ASIDE

We very much believe that children need role models. So do parents. Think about your children and the role models for parenting that they might see on television. For our parents' generation, the consensus role models seemed to be Mr. and Mrs. Cleaver and Ozzie and Harriet. Of course, it was easier to be a parent in a perfect world—or at least near-perfect—which was where Ozzie and Harriet lived. They were never exposed to drugs or some of the other modern perils that beset today's children and grandchildren. And we could argue that the worlds we see on television aren't realistic at all, and so the question is pointless. Still, the next time you see your children having problems being parents, remember that it was never easy for you either, and they might have to rely on you as parenting role models instead of what they see on TV. That's okay, you've done a great job with raising your children, and you have the wonderful advantage of hindsight. So, when it comes to parenting, show them how! Note that they'll absorb more if you show—*not tell*—them how.

WHILE YOU'RE WATCHING A PARADE:

▶ At some point in the past, people commemorated the return of wartime soldiers with parades. This seems to have fallen out of favor. Talk about this with your grandchildren.

▶ Ask them to pick out their favorite float or event. Why is it their favorite?

▶ Do your grandchildren want to get some of their friends together and have their own parade? What would they like their parade to commemorate?

▶ What is confetti? Maybe they would like to make their own confetti for their parade. (Of course, keep the cleaning-up process afterward in mind.)

▶ Explain what a "ticker tape" parade is. (Ticker tape is the print-out of stock prices on narrow paper that was thrown from office building windows, usually in lower Manhattan.)

P
A
R
A
D
E
S

COMPUTER SHOW

Fun Fact

The IBM personal computer
was introduced in 1981.

If you don't live near a large city, you might have to drive a while to find a computer show. When we did, we thoroughly enjoyed the experience. Even if you don't buy anything, having all the computers around gives you lots of things to think about. What types of software and add-ons did you want the most? There was one booth in particular that we found fascinating—the voice-recognition software package. They demonstrated it by having someone talk, and while he was doing so, the screen behind him showed the computer writing down everything he said.

This can really inspire a young grandchild into an interest in science or technology. This practical way to pass along advice to the youngsters is a way of showing—not telling. For those of us on a tight budget, there are usually bargain bins containing slightly outdated gaming software available for purchase. Before you buy anything, make sure you know the basics of your grandchild's computer, because most software requires certain versions of an operating system.

A GRANDPARENT ASIDE

Many families today are suffering financially. If your grandchildren are old enough to get a job and want to chip in and earn a few bucks for the family pot, that's great. Not only will your grandchild feel like a contributing member to the family, but jobs can teach responsibility—although you should certainly have a talk about the best ways to spend money, and buying an eighty-dollar pair of jeans isn't necessarily it. It can be difficult to allow grandchildren to chip in. This can be due to something as simple as pride. But the benefits to the grandchildren will be great. One time we were at a store and had left some of our money at home. We didn't notice until we were at the checkout counter. The benefits became obvious to us when one of our grandchildren chipped in a couple of quarters, and we realized how important the sense of contributing is to young children. It helps give them a sense that they are valued members of the family.

WHILE YOU'RE AT A COMPUTER SHOW:

▶ Do your grandchildren know what an abacus is? How about a slide rule?

▶ Can they explain how to use a computer? Prompt them to show you so that you can understand better.

▶ If they could write a computer program to do anything possible, what would they write?

▶ Begin a discussion about the computer that beat the world chess champion. Does this mean that computers are smarter than people? Does a computer have intelligence?

HIKING AND NATURE PHOTOGRAPHY

Fun Fact

The first Polaroid camera was
sold to the public in November, 1948.

Adding a camera to your nature hike can add a new dimension to your walk. We suggest going to a bookstore beforehand to check out the coffee table books. There are usually books with big pictures or nature shots. Now, when you're on a hike, you can challenge your grandchildren to take some pictures like those. While it helps to have a camera capable of close-ups, this isn't necessary. We've had a lot of success with one-use disposable cameras. Decide beforehand if you're going to take pictures of trees or smaller plants. We suggest taking a short drive to a nearby park and a hiking trail. But if you'd prefer to stay closer to home, take a hike through the neighborhood and take pictures of neighborhood pets. In the springtime, all of the flowers are in bloom. Your grandchildren will learn that while it looks easy to take those wonderful pictures you see in those coffee table books, capturing the beauty of nature is a hard task!

Who knows—maybe this will lead to assignments in their school newspapers or a photojournalism job.

A GRANDPARENT ASIDE

When your grandchildren have aged a bit and are old enough to have friends of their own, having their friends over for dinner or playtime will allow you to observe how they interact. Do they laugh and joke and monkey around? Do they have serious, in-depth political discussions? Can they spend ten minutes without someone saying something silly? We have a spare room that can be called a recreation room. This is a special room that we allow our grandchildren to use with their friends. Of course, we check on them often! It's a good place for us as grandparents to see what their friends are like when they let their guard down. Even when they're not in the rec room, it's a good idea to keep an eye on their friends. Watch for anything they might suggest they're involved with something dangerous such as alcohol or drugs. We want to protect our grandchildren as much as possible by knowing the company they keep.

WHILE YOU'RE HIKING
AND TAKING NATURE PICTURES:

▶ Do they ever look through magazines? What was the last one they read that had nature pictures?

▶ How many different regions of the world can they name? Any deserts? The Antarctic? How about the Serengeti plains?

▶ Ask them to explain light and color to you. If they don't know, have them investigate and report back to you on the next visit.

NURSING HOME

Fun Fact

There are over 18,000 nursing home in the United States, with over 1.9 million beds.

This activity teaches grandchildren that the act of giving brings many rewards to the giver, not just to the recipient of the gift—and that sometimes the greatest gift is the gift of time. Many times grandchildren grow up with a "what's in it for me" attitude. Well, it is true that sometimes community service gets the short end of the stick. If this sparks their interest, there are many volunteer services that a child can join once they are older, but what we're referring to now is taking an afternoon, or even a spare hour, and visiting a nursing home. Make sure to call ahead to talk to the people in charge and let them know you're coming. They usually will have some ideas to help you spend your visit. We suggest having your grandchildren read to someone, or offer to write a letter for them. Are they interested in playing a card game? Have your grandchildren ask the elderly what *they* would like to do.

A GRANDPARENT ASIDE

Think about the expression "laugh it off." It's definitely a good thing to be able to laugh off some of the things that happened when we were children and parents. Most doctors agree laughing is healthy. It relieves stress and helps maintain a healthy frame of mind. And most people who are looking for an ideal mate will say a sense of humor is important. So, take the time to laugh at some of the more inopportune events that happen in our lives—especially with our grandchildren. The next time your grandchildren are over for the weekend, rent a funny movie or tell a joke. Get your grandkids to laugh with you.

WHILE YOU'RE AT THE NURSING HOME:

▶ Can you get any of the residents to talk to your grandchildren about the things they remember most about growing up? Ask for stories.

▶ On the way back, ask your grandchildren to recall everything they can about the visit. Will they tell their parents?

▶ Tell them about some of the stories you've heard about people who are brave in the face of injury and sickness.

▶ Did they enjoy the visit? What did they like or dislike?

7

LONG TRIPS

▼

WHILE YOU CAN have a lot of fun on a short trip, longer trips give you many more options. These require time to plan, but are always worthwhile, and they have a much greater chance of being remembered by your grandchildren. The captive audience while you're in the car driving to your destination is great, too. There can be so many distractions at home, from television and portable music players to telephones and chores. But when you're all in the car for a few hours, you will have plenty of time to get into deep discussions. Grandkids are quick to answer "Fine" to the question "How was your day?" But now's your chance to take the time to dig a little deeper:

"What was fine about it?"

"Tell me three things one of your teachers told you yesterday."

"Tell me the names of the people you talk to during the day."

As you read through this book, you'll find lots of topics to discuss during one of these long trips. And if you run out of conversation topics, play "I Spy!"

DID YOU KNOW?

We've heard the phrase "just be yourself" so many times, and it's still great advice. It's the standard answer to questions on how to act in a stressful situation, from a first date to attending a new school. Most people can recognize when someone else is not acting like themselves, and it doesn't make a good first impression. But this advice may not help a child that doesn't yet know who they are. A good way to help your grandchildren develop this is to act out role-playing scenarios. For example, ask your grandchild to pretend for a few minutes to be someone who always says something wrong, always exaggerates, gets sad very easily, or is always grinning because they are happy every minute of the day. Then, they will take this personality and play the role of a boss at work, a prince trying to win a princess's hand in marriage, or a schoolteacher. Then you will play another role, such as employee, the princess, the student in class. Your job is to stir up the pot by asking questions and pushing the boundaries of your role (for example, a princess who wants to abandon her royal status). This can be fun, and it will help your grandchild to heed the advice, "Be yourself."

MORE INFORMATION: BOOKS

Berman, Jenn and Donna Corwin. *The A to Z Guide to Raising Happy, Confident Kids.* New World Library. Novato, California: 2007.
This book is a quick read that answers the most frequently asked questions about how to raise a healthy, well-adjusted child.

Coloroso, Barbara. *Kids Are Worth It! Revised Edition: Giving Your Child the Gift of Inner Discipline.* Collins. New York: 2002.
This book uses a combination of compassion and respect while disciplining to teach limits without damaging the child's self-esteem.

Loomans, Diane and Julia Loomans. *100 Ways to Build Self-Esteem and Teach Values*. HJ Kramer/New World Library. Novato, California: 2003.

The activities in this book are designed to promote love and self-worth, and a bond between parent and child.

McFarlane. Penny. *Dramatherapy: Developing Emotional Stability*. David Fulton Publishers. London: 2006.

The British Association of Dramatherapists has given its definition of dramatherapy as having as its main focus the "intentional use of the healing aspects of drama and theatre as the therapeutic process."

More Information: Websites

www.kidsource.com/kidsource/content2/Strengthen_Children_Self.html

A short article on aspects of how to raise a child's self-esteem.

www.loveourchildrenusa.org/teachingkidsselfesteem.php

Includes tips and strategies for dealing with a child's self-esteem, including warnings about overdoing it and how to deal with overweight children.

www.4children.org/news/102pare.htm

From the Action Alliance for Children, an article that talks about programs for parents to improve parenting skills.

DAIRY FARM

Fun Fact

The average cow in the United States produces about 6.2 gallons of milk per day, and the U.S. has over 100 million cattle and calves, according to the USDA.

We remember taking school trips to dairy farms when we were younger. It was all part of a good education! Nowadays, when you ask a kid where the grocery store milk comes from (go ahead and try!), they might answer a cow, but how many have actually seen the process? We believe in helping our grandchildren feel more connected to the world in which they live, and knowing—and seeing—where their food comes from is a good start to that. Ask to see the henhouses, and perhaps spot a few eggs. Make sure you ask them what section of the grocery store you can find these products in. (The *dairy* section! Doh!) As usual, bring those cameras! If a dairy farm isn't available, any farm will serve well to teach grandkids about food products. Check chambers of commerce in nearby farming communities for visiting opportunities.

A GRANDPARENTING ASIDE

We've heard it said that it's a grandparent's right, if not outright obligation, to spoil the grandchildren. Let's knock off that particular nonsense right here and now. Sure, we love buying gifts for our grandchildren. However, we also know of grandparents who buy expensive stuff daily, so much that there are dressers full of clothes that will never be worn and every birthday and Christmas has the parents scratching their heads because they can't think of any toy that the kid will enjoy more than the $400 toy ATVs in the driveway. We know some parents who are unnecessarily stressed out on their children's birthdays because they cannot compete financially with the grandparents. This often extends to the holiday season. It's a good idea to talk to your children and come to an agreement as to what makes sense, price-wise, for gifts for the grandkids.

WHILE YOU'RE AT A DAIRY FARM:

▶ Talk to the farmhands. What do they do? Prompt your grand-children to think of questions to ask on the drive in.

▶ Did you know any farmers when you were growing up? Tell your grandchildren about them!

▶ What sorts of tools do you see around? Do your grandchildren know the uses of all of these? Have them guess if they don't already know, and then ask someone and see how close you are.

▶ Are there any cows out grazing? Ask a farmhand when the cows come home. (It's usually dusk.)

TUBING

Water tubing is a great summer activity! It's not a high-action activity. If it sounds like too much exercise, you're thinking about rivers that move too fast. Tubing takes place on a nice, lazy river. There are many places that will come and pick you up at prearranged locations after an hour or two of floating down a river, and they'll rent you a tube, too. Call your local chamber of commerce or look online for tubing opportunities in your area. Before you're ready to go, make sure everybody is wearing waterproof sunscreen. The sun can be brutal when you're exposed on a river. If you're interested in doing this by yourself, look for a place that has a wide curve in a river. You put yourself into the river, float for ten minutes around the curve, then take a short walk back to the start and put yourself in again. If you have your own tube, you can protect skin from the valve stem by wrapping waterproof tape around the innertube. Always take some bottled water with you so nobody gets in danger of dehydration. And don't forget to wear life jackets!

A GRANDPARENT ASIDE

When you go for long-distance trips, it's always a good idea to have a first-aid kit nearby. You can find travel kits that are pre-assembled and are fairly reasonably priced in many discount stores. Carry one around in your car. When a grandchild's finger gets scratched and you have ointment and a Band-Aid on hand, you'll come across as wise and prepared (which, of course, you are!) This will reinforce the grandchildren's notion that they should pay heed to your advice (which, of course, they should!). If you would rather assemble a first-aid kit yourself, they are easily assembled. All you need is a Zip-Loc bag to hold the items, or you can find a small craft or sewing box. We suggest including adhesive bandages, a children's fever reducer (such as Children's Tylenol), a children's thermometer (typically digital, these days), a medicine dispenser (dropper or spoon-type, depending on the ages of children), smiley-face stickers for being brave, and instant ice packs, which can help reduce swelling for those twisted and turned ankles and other joints. If you plan to take it tubing or on any water activity, make sure the package floats and is waterproof. Try doubling your Zip-Loc bag to keep it afloat.

WHILE YOU'RE TUBING:

▶ Paddle with your hand so you are spinning in circles. Get your grandchildren to emulate you.

▶ Play bumper-cars and "crash" into them, feigning a great, jarring collision.

▶ Do they notice any unusual birds or wildlife?

▶ Hang outside your tube, holding it with your hands ahead of you (instead of sitting in it), and paddle with your legs for extra propulsion (and exercise!).

WINDSURFING

Fun Fact

The very first windsurfing patent ever was granted in 1970.

Even if you are not as athletically inclined as you once were, there are windsurfing boards made for you! If you're a windsurfing newbie, we strongly suggest taking lessons with your grandchildren. We've found that a good starting age for grandchildren is around 7 or 8 years old; their coordination has developed enough that they have the necessary sense of balance. The first day, you might only get out in the water after an hour or two of instruction, but it'll be worth it. And the next time, you'll be ready to go. We were only able to stay on a windsurfing board a few seconds the first time before falling, slipping, or otherwise losing our balance and plunging into the water. Always wear life preservers and surf only in water deeper than chest level. The boards are usually fiberglass, and it's possible to hit your head on the edge of the board. But that's usually the least of your problems. First, you must stand upright. (It might not be such a great idea to bring the cameras to this activity; there are too many opportunities for embarrassing photos.) Once you get the swing of it, you can take pictures. If you never catch on, perhaps your grandchildren will. If so, it'll be a skill they'll carry with them the rest of their lives.

A GRANDPARENTING ASIDE

Don't be self-conscious about yourself or the way you look with your grandchildren. Grandchildren accept you for the way you are, so why shouldn't you? If you're worried about how you will look in swimwear, take some time to go shopping and pick out clothing that will give you freedom of movement. If you're worried about weight issues or getting sunburn, get a swimsuit that covers a lot of skin. Other than that, you shouldn't worry about it. Your grandchildren certainly don't. And you shouldn't worry about what anybody else thinks, either, because we're focused on the grandkids, right?

WHILE YOU'RE WINDSURFING:

▶ Have your grandchildren ever been sunburned?

▶ What does SPF mean? (sun proctective factor)

▶ What muscles are being exercised during windsurfing? (Practically all of them! This will explain why you're so sore afterward.)

▶ Would they like to go on a sailboat one day?

▶ Has anybody ever sailed all the way around the world? Can they name anyone? (Yes, many! In fact, there's an annual race.)

BOOGIE BOARDING

Fun Fact

"Boogie" is a name brand of bodyboards. Bodyboarding is the earliest form of wave surfing, with historic references as early as 1778!

If you're near the beach, you might be lucky and find some other Boogie boarders. Watch them to see how it's done. In brief: you'll need a shallow sheet of water to ride the waves successfully. Stand in the sand near the shoreline. We find that when a wave comes into shore, just before it starts to recede, there's a thin sheet of water. Place the Boogie board on this shallow sheet of water and jump on with a little forward momentum. (It's like a short surfing ride on 2 inches of water.) We've had horrible luck with being successful ourselves, but we had fun trying. And we certainly entertained our grandchildren in the process! If you're looking for a place to purchase your board, most department stores carry them. You can also rent one at a beach shop. Remember that it's easy to get dehydrated (see if the grandkids know what that word means!), so bring along some water and make sure your grandchildren drink plenty.

A GRANDPARENT ASIDE

Be available. Let them know your email address and phone number. Let them know that they can talk to you about anything they want. Grandparents can have different kinds of relationships with their grandchildren, but friendship should be one aspect of them. Grandchildren (as well as everyone else) can change friends from year to year, and they can often have feelings that nobody understands them. Be supportive and available by talking to them often. They might need to call you at some point with a problem that's troubling them.

WHILE YOU'RE BOOGIE BOARDING:

▶ Have your grandchildren ever skipped stones across water? Try it at a lake to see who can make the most skips!

▶ Would they like to make a sand castle?

▶ Have they ever gone hunting for shells and interesting rocks? Take them after you're finished with Boogie boarding.

▶ Challenge them to spot a minnow or other fish.

TOUR

Fun Fact

The first colonial lighthouse was established in 1716, on Little Brewster Island, on Boston Harbor in Massachusetts.

We live about a four-hour drive from the coast, so it's a long trip for us, but not out of the question to take a day and tour a lighthouse. We suggest going on a temperate day, because most lighthouses do not have air conditioning. (Or elevators!) Lighthouses hold a special meaning to us, and they are indeed filled with history and lore, but you might find something equally intriguing much closer to home. How about the arch in St. Louis? The Space Needle in Seattle? The Grand Canyon? There are plenty of monuments and other sights that are a long (but doable) drive from your home. Remember to bring those cameras and make sure you talk about the trip well in advance with your grandchildren. This will help build up their excitement. Remember to have a deep conversation while you're en route, which will allow you to remark to yourselves, "My, how they've matured since we saw them last!"

A GRANDPARENT ASIDE

Financial understanding (how to balance a checkbook, the miracle of compound interest, how much you'd have in retirement if you'd saved 10 dollars a week in a 401k) is usually taught by the parents, but you as grandparents often have a wider perspective on it because you've been around longer. Youngsters' knowledge of money and finances are really neglected these days. Telling them that money doesn't grow on trees won't help; they do know that. But, if they're given everything they ask for, and never have to save money for something they want and earn that money by doing chores, they might never get a sense of how finances work. Walk them through this process by opening a savings account for them. Take them to the bank and have them deposit money into it. Keep the records in a special drawer at your place, and go over it occasionally with your grandchildren.

WHILE YOU'RE ON THE TOUR:

▶ What do your grandchildren know about the history of the tour site? If you don't know, ask someone or find a brochure.

▶ Ask what kind of monument or tour attraction they would like to see built. How about you?

▶ Talk about any of the monuments, tour sites, or other attractions that you might have seen that have special meaning for you.

▶ Can they name any of the monuments or tour attractions in Washington, D.C.?

I SPY

Fun Fact

The TV show *I Spy* ran from 1965 to 1968, and was Bill Cosby's big acting breakthrough. He won numerous Emmys for his role on the show.

It's a good idea to know the basic rules of popular games to play during long drives. "I Spy" is certainly one of them. You might see a bus and say, "I spy something yellow." The person who names the bus wins and gets to go next, spying something. In "20 questions'" you envision an object and players can ask 20 questions to identify it, answerable only by "yes" and "no." (This is where the famous phrase "Is it bigger than a breadbox?" comes from.) At one point, there was a popular TV game show based on the game. Look online for more games to play while driving. You can play a form of bingo based on numbers on license plates that you spot. "Slug Bug" is a big HIT when you spot a Volkswagen. And of course, there's always singing. The problem is finding a song that everybody knows the words to. Good luck!

A GRANDPARENT ASIDE

Grandparents have accumulated a lot of knowledge about the world. We have great experience with how things work and why people do the things they do. It only makes sense that we would want to impart that knowledge to our grandchildren, to give them an edge and help them not make the same mistakes we made. We're all for that! However, in general, think about the amount of time you spend listening to your grandchildren during conversations. Is it fifty percent of the time? Ten percent? (We're fairly sure none of us can withstand ninety percent.) Listening is just as important as imparting your wisdom. Shoot for fifty percent.

WHILE YOU'RE DRIVING:

▶ Make sure you point out how meaningless it is to win any of these games. The whole point of them is to interact and have fun!

▶ What other long trips have you taken?

▶ What was the longest trip your grandchildren can remember? What did they do on it?

▶ Ask everyone about the one (or more) place they want to visit in the next five years.

I

S

P

Y

ALL FRIENDS ARE INVITED!

▼

I T'S GREAT TO have one-on-one time with your grandchildren. It can also be just as much fun to have them to bring over some of their friends. You'll get to see who they hang out with, and their friends will get to meet a great grandparent—you! These are group activities designed to entertain your grandchildren and their friends. Don't feel as if you need to jump through hoops to appear to be the coolest grandparents on the block, but it would be a great thing if your grandchildren were able to talk about the time they spent with you while at school with their friends. So, the next time you're talking to your grandchildren, check to see if their friends would like to visit, too. As always, double-check with the parents and make sure this is allowed.

DID YOU KNOW?

Maybe it's just that sex offenses make the national news much more often these days, but it seems to us that there are more predators out there than ever. There is greater information available in recent years tracking and locating sexual predators. While we don't want to get into the politics of the matter, we do think it's a good idea to be aware if there are any convicted predators in the neighborhood. As with many other aspects in life, knowledge is power. And you'll find yourself better armed the more knowledge you have. Depending on the ages of your grandchildren, you might want to tell them about how many sexual offenders live in your area. We were astonished by the large number in our small town.

MORE INFORMATION: BOOKS

De Becker, Gavin. *Protecting the Gift: Keeping Children and Teenagers Safe (and Parents Sane).* Dell. New York: 2000.

This book offers practical advice on recognizing signs of danger to children and how to teach children about potential risks without scaring them.

Giammarinaro, James. *Parents, Predators, and Prevention.* Pelican Press. Aptos, California: 2006.

This book is a great guide to learning about abductors and how they operate, and what parents and grandparents can do to prevent your child from becoming a victim.

Jackson, Joyce and Preston Jones. *How to Protect Your Child from Sexual Predators.* Keeping Kids Safe, Inc. Walnut Creek, California: 2007.

Outlines methods for protecting children against online threats.

Smith, Gregory C. *How to Protect Your Children on the Internet: A Road Map for Parents and Teachers.* Praeger Publishers. Westport, Connecticut: 2007.

A concise book that explains ways to protect children from online threats.

More Information: Websites

www.yellodyno.com

A website for parents and educators with information on protecting children (ages 4 to 12) from being victimized by various offenders such as abductors, bullies, and Internet predators.

www.stopsexoffenders.com

Includes a free search for locations of registered sex offenders.

www.saferchildren.net

Informative and educational website focusing on the psychology of child predators.

www.stopchildpredators.org

Goals include creating federal policy changes to protect victims. Includes a free newsletter.

www.amw.com

The site of America's Most Wanted. Has list of AMBER Alerts and a crime hotline phone number.

www.pollyklaas.org

Web home of the Polly Klaas Foundation, focusing on missing children. Includes free newsletter.

COOKOUT

Your grandchildren may already be familiar with cookouts thrown by their parents. Doesn't matter: a cookout with the grandparents is a whole new ballgame! It's important for grandchildren to be exposed to different ways of doing things, different meals, and different rules of etiquette. The parents might insist on cutting a hot dog with a knife and fork, but you hold it with your hands. How about an ear of corn? Different people eat differently. Maybe show them how to grill with charcoal—they might have only seen gas grills. Better yet, make a campfire, take out your old camping equipment, and make a meal over a real fire. (We do this very simply with hot dogs on sticks and beans cooked in their can.) Many local parks have grills. All you need to supply is charcoal, lighter, and grub!

A GRANDPARENT ASIDE

Grandparents become primary caregivers for many reasons, from incarceration to the death of parents to plain old financial inability. For whatever reason, the number of grandparents who are primary caregivers for their grandchildren is growing at a rapid rate. If you're not in this situation yourself, chances are you know somebody who is. Going down the "parenting route" a second time as you approach retirement can be overwhelming, but there are many organizations that can help. One of the most effective places to look is the AARP (Association for the Advancement of Retired Persons). Membership for the AARP begins at age 50, so it's for people approaching retirement, as well as retired folks. They have provided "one-stop" help for grandparents who become primary caregivers. Check out their website (use a library computer if you need to) at www.aarp.org.

WHILE YOU'RE COOKING OUT:

► How does heat kill germs and bacteria? (Heat causes chemical reactions, destroying molecules such as DNA.)

► Why should you be careful of eating uncooked food (such as undercooked chicken)? (Thorough cooking ensures the destruction of dangerous bacteria such as *E. coli*.)

► Do astronauts cook their meals? (Because oxygen is a scarce resource in space, cooking over open flames is very likely a big no-no.)

► What would your grandchildren like to have on the menu for the next cookout?

TREASURE MAP

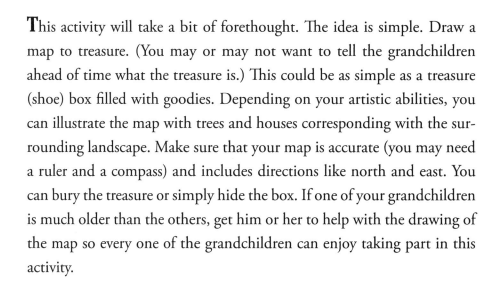

Fun Fact

The oldest known maps are on Babylonian clay
tablets dating from about 2300 B.C.

This activity will take a bit of forethought. The idea is simple. Draw a
map to treasure. (You may or may not want to tell the grandchildren
ahead of time what the treasure is.) This could be as simple as a treasure
(shoe) box filled with goodies. Depending on your artistic abilities, you
can illustrate the map with trees and houses corresponding with the sur-
rounding landscape. Make sure that your map is accurate (you may need
a ruler and a compass) and includes directions like north and east. You
can bury the treasure or simply hide the box. If one of your grandchildren
is much older than the others, get him or her to help with the drawing of
the map so every one of the grandchildren can enjoy taking part in this
activity.

A GRANDPARENT ASIDE

Every grandparent wants to help their grandchild grow up healthy and bright. One of the biggest things you can do to help develop your grandchild's intelligence is to encourage them to ask questions. That's one of the reasons we list conversation starters for each activity. If there's just one thing you can do to provide an excellent foundation, it is to increase the number of questions that are asked (either by you or the grandchildren) and answered. For many of our questions, there are no simple answers. For example, what is the best way to ensure that most people have health insurance? We don't want to paint ourselves as moral relativists, but on the other hand, the world is full of questions whose answers are varied shades of gray.

WHILE YOU'RE HUNTING FOR TREASURE:

▶ Why did pirates bury their treasure? (So it wouldn't get stolen, and they couldn't very well put it in a bank, could they?)

▶ Why does gold stand up so well over time in buried treasure? (Because gold does not tarnish or decay.)

▶ What is the difference between true north and magnetic north? (Compasses point to magnetic north, which is in a slightly different location from the top of the axis about which the earth spins.)

▶ Why are maps so important when going on a long-distance road trip?

ALL FRIENDS ARE INVITED!

T R E A S U R E M A P

JOGGING

If you're into fitness, this is a great way to pass on some of your healthy habits to your grandchildren. Have you seen those movies such as *Stripes* with Bill Murray in which Army recruits chant as their platoons jog across the base? That's the idea here. Sing one word every time a shoe hits the ground. Here's our chant:

> We are the joggers
> The mighty, mighty joggers,
> Everywhere we go oh,
> People want to know oh,
> who we are
> so we tell 'em
> We are the joggers
> (and so on)

Come up with your own chants, or replace the word "joggers" in the chant we use! Or just count to four repeatedly with each step. If you're not quite up to jogging, you can walk and have your grandchildren walk or jog, depending on their age and experience. You can drive to a park (bring plenty of water if you do) or simply go through your neighborhood. Remember to loosen up those limbs and stretch beforehand! If you're not sure how to properly stretch, ask around at a gym or speak directly with your grandchildren's physical education instructors.

A GRANDPARENTING ASIDE

One of our inside jokes' punch lines is "Take a hike!" The lead-up to this is often a question that asks for advice on raising a child. We suggest to literally get up, leave the house, and take a hike. This will relieve stress and help you feel better about many troublesome situations. Stress has become such a large factor in the day-to-day care of children and grandchildren. Sometimes it's easy to start taking everything the wrong way, allowing all of the little daily pressures to build up until the pot boils over. When your grandchildren's parents are going through a rough stretch, suggest a short walk with the kids after dinner to reawaken those bonds between them. It's great exercise, and it will stimulate conversation. It will take them away from the TV, too. We stroll on the same route, which keeps the focus on the conversation. Children might like exploring on their walks instead, and that's fine—whatever works. Just get outside and get those legs moving.

WHILE YOU'RE CHANTING AND JOGGING:

▶ Have they ever seen long-distance runners in marathons or during the Olympics on TV?

- ▶ What kinds of exercise do they get at school and at home?
- ▶ Tell them about some of the most physically strenuous endeavors you've done in your life.
- ▶ Have they ever seen workout videos on TV?

BALLOON ANIMALS

Fun Fact

Balloon-A-Palooza 2006 had more than 110,000 balloons and 12,000 attendees!

We're sure you've seen people, maybe at a circus or a birthday party, creating these fun toys for giveaways. Long, thin balloons (usually somewhat under-inflated) are stretched and twisted around until there's an animal, often resembling a stick figure. We remember the dogs the best. You can look online or check out books from the library for techniques. There are also kits sold at toy stores and even some bookstore chains. The great thing about this activity is that your grandchildren and their friends will have mementos to bring home with them. A brief word of caution: You don't want to create balloons for children who are too young to know not to place the balloons in their mouths. This is very dangerous; children have died from balloons popping in their mouths and blocking their airways. It's also good to talk about how small plastic toys can block breathing airways.

A GRANDPARENTING ASIDE

Keep up with family reunions. If none are scheduled, try setting one up yourself. We feel that these should be annual events. Many times parents are overwhelmed with work and child care. Any spare time they get is used to refresh their batteries so they can survive another grinding week at work (this includes homemakers). Try to accommodate as many schedules as you can, then set aside a weekend (or more) in the summer and host a family reunion. Not everybody will make it, and maybe they will just drop by for an hour or two. That's fine. It's the tradition of the reunion that's important. And it'll be a tradition that your grandchildren will carry on with their own children.

WHILE YOU'RE MAKING BALLOON FIGURES:

▶ See who can make the tallest balloon figure that can stand up on its own.

▶ Why do some balloons rise? (They are filled with helium or heated air or some other lighter-than-air gas.)

▶ Give your balloon figures names.

▶ Do they have any teachers or parents who would like a balloon figure as a gift?

WATER BALLOONS

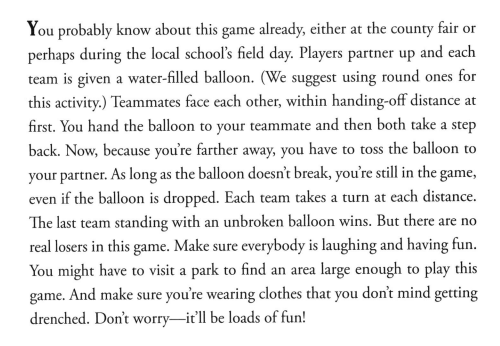

Fun Fact

The first rubber balloons were made by Professor Michael Faraday in 1824 to use in his experiments with hydrogen.

You probably know about this game already, either at the county fair or perhaps during the local school's field day. Players partner up and each team is given a water-filled balloon. (We suggest using round ones for this activity.) Teammates face each other, within handing-off distance at first. You hand the balloon to your teammate and then both take a step back. Now, because you're farther away, you have to toss the balloon to your partner. As long as the balloon doesn't break, you're still in the game, even if the balloon is dropped. Each team takes a turn at each distance. The last team standing with an unbroken balloon wins. But there are no real losers in this game. Make sure everybody is laughing and having fun. You might have to visit a park to find an area large enough to play this game. And make sure you're wearing clothes that you don't mind getting drenched. Don't worry—it'll be loads of fun!

A GRANDPARENT ASIDE

There's usually a time when the subject of teachers comes up. If it doesn't come up in normal conversation, make it a point to raise it yourself. Talk about some of the teachers that you remember from when you were in school. Teachers play an important role in the lives of many children, and it's good to understand what your grandchildren think of theirs. Did you have any teachers that challenged you? Did any help you figure out what you wanted to do in life? Maybe you had a teacher who was very strict, and it wasn't until later that you developed an appreciation for what they did for you. This perspective helps grandparents be some of the best teachers around!

WHILE YOU'RE TOSSING WATER BALLOONS:

- ▶ Take two or three balloons and try to juggle them. See who can do the most juggles without dropping a balloon.
- ▶ How many different ways can they catch or throw a balloon? What about underhand, or catching with one hand?
- ▶ Would they like to switch partners? Suggest drawing straws for partners.
- ▶ How high can everybody throw a balloon and catch it without it breaking?

BIKING

Fun Fact

The most efficient animal on earth in terms of weight transported over distance for energy expended is a human on a bicycle.

Bicycling is great on quiet neighborhood roads. Make sure you tell your grandkids that the road rules apply to bicyclists, too! They are required to stop at all stop signs and signal to turn. Make sure you are aware of the safety laws in your state, from helmets to kneepads. Regardless of legal requirements, we strongly urge that helmets be worn, and smaller children will benefit from knee pads. The object isn't to race or to cover a great distance. A quiet ride with grandchildren and friends is great exercise, and it also is a great way to promote conversation. It's wonderful how cool the breeze is, too, even though you're exerting energy and quite possibly sweating. So, talk over the safety rules with everybody before you head out. Then take a spin around the block and have a great ride.

A GRANDPARENT ASIDE

It seems like there was a time when asking for support was frowned upon. Nobody liked to admit to needing advice, and sometimes a stigma was attached to the family of an alcoholic or a gambler. But support groups can be wonderful, not only for grandparents, but for parents. If your adult children are coming to you with problems, you can suggest they research support groups in the area to find help and a community of people with similar problems. If you're feeling overburdened because you find yourself as primary caregivers for grandchildren, remember that you're part of a growing segment of society—and you're not alone. So get some support for you and your children, the grandchildren's parents. It's a tough world out there, and there's no shame in looking for a little help.

WHILE YOU'RE BICYCLING:

▶ Talk about a bicycle you rode as a youngster.

▶ Would they like to get any bicycle accessories, such as a water bottle and holder? How about a speedometer?

▶ Do they know how to install it on their bike?

▶ What is so important about proper tire pressure? (If the tires are under-inflated, it's so much more difficult to pedal.)

▶ What does "draft" mean? (When you ride directly behind someone, who blocks the wind and makes it an easier ride.)

B
I
K
I
N
G

RACING

Fun Fact

A pig running at top speed can run
a mile in about 7.5 minutes.

This is a great game for younger children (not necessarily the grandparents, although we don't want to exclude you if you are up for it), especially when friends are over. Around the house makes for a natural racecourse. It's roughly oval and has lots of obstacles (garage, trees, even woodsheds). If you feel that one lap isn't enough, go for five. While the quicker children might win the shorter race, those with endurance can win the longer races. We admit we do have several ulterior motives with this activity. It's a great activity for getting your grandchildren exhausted and ready for their bath and bed. Plus, it's fun. Get out those checkered flags and start a race around your house this evening!

A GRANDPARENT ASIDE

While we believe that routines are very important during your grandchildren's nurturing, diversity is an important aspect of their lives as well. While this might sound like a paradox, it's not. When the grandchildren are with their parents, routines like bedtime and mealtimes help give them a sense of security. But when they see the differences in how Uncle Bob serves meals and how Aunt Mary gets ready for bed, this widens their perspective. Expanding children's horizons is essential to helping them become independent, successful adults.

WHILE YOU'RE RACING AROUND THE HOUSE:

▶ Have your grandchildren ever thought about track and field?

▶ Can they list any of the running events in high school? (The 100, 200, and 400 meter dashes. The 3000 meter run. The 110 meter high hurdles.)

▶ Have they ever heard of the Boston Marathon? (It's 26 miles long!)

▶ Ask them if they'd like to hear about any running you have done in your life.

▶ Do they know about how the process of sweating (and the evaporation of the sweat) cools the human body? (The heat needed to turn liquid sweat into water vapor is released into the air, leaving the skin cooler.)

SLEEPOVER!

Fun Fact

Pajamas were introduced in India in 1880 for men to wear instead of nightshirts.

Throwing a sleepover with the grandchildren's friends is not a simple task and may be asking a lot of you. It will require a lot of your time, and you're going to have to check on them throughout the night to be sure there's no mischief going on. You will also have to plan for meals and snacks, and most importantly, you are going to have to make sure that the other parents are all on the same page with the plans. Make sure you have phone numbers of the families of everyone who is attending, in case of emergency. This can be a great activity, and definitely will be a memorable one for your grandchildren. They'll be able to talk to their friends while at school and bring you into the conversation because of the time you have all spent together. That is worth the time and effort.

A GRANDPARENT ASIDE

While we don't want to be the ones to raise any sore spots, we felt this would be good to mention. Sometimes our children take advantage of the grandparent-babysitting-service, and it's easy to do so because we're keen on watching the grandchildren. Parenting is tough work, as you well know. In times past, grandparents lived under the same roof and there were three generations to help out. We do understand how tempting it is to rely on the grandparents to watch the grandkids. This habit may start out with you taking care of them on the weekends, and then one night during the week . . . then, before you know it, you have the kids more than the parents, as they're zooming off on business and personal trips out of state. Learn how to say "no," and don't feel guilty about it. In the long run, it might save your relationship with your children.

WHILE YOU'RE HOSTING A SLEEPOVER:

▶ Tell everybody a story from your youth.

▶ Are there any games that the friends know and want to play?

▶ Make sure you ask the friends about their lives so that you understand the relationship between them and your grandchildren.

▶ Does anyone have any scary stories or jokes to share?

IN THE TOY TRUNK

SOMETIMES WE OVERLOOK the spare minutes we have during the day. For example, you're on the road going to pick up a friend of your grandchildren who ends up running late. You spend ten minutes in the driveway waiting. The same thing can happen when dropping the grandkids off for practice, whether it's sports, music, or drama, and the instructor or coach is late. These ten minutes are a unique opportunity to bond further with your grandkids. You could, of course, just talk; but wouldn't that talk be easier if you were doing an activity to help them open up?

This chapter provides those activities and tips you can use when you have a few extra minutes in your car. We suggest buying a storage tub (a toy trunk!) to hold the materials, such as binoculars for bird watching and books. Keep a copy of this book there, too!

DID YOU KNOW?

Television has advanced a great deal since we were kids. One of the biggest differences is how realistic the TV shows are today. There's even an entirely new genre of "reality" shows. Some studies have indicated that, because of this, it might be more difficult for children to know what's real and what's made up. A good way to teach children about movies being "make-believe" is to rent some old classic B movies. Do you remember how scared you were when you first saw *Journey to the Center of the Earth* or *The Creature from the Black Lagoon?* By today's standards, the special effects are comical. Because they are so obvious, they are a useful tool to teach how movie makers pull off those unbelievable stunts. Sit down with your grandchildren and explain things like outtakes, stuntmen, and make-up that adds bruises to people's faces. There have been far too many children who have died mimicking what they saw on TV. The silver screen doesn't get off free here either; many kids have gotten injured copying stunts from a movie. Take some time during your movie night or cartoon mornings to explain how much of what they see on television is choreographed.

MORE INFORMATION: BOOKS

Bryant, Jennings and J. Alison Bryant. *Television and the American Family.* Lawrence Erlbaum. Mahwah, NJ: 2000.

Feedback and information on the interaction between families and the television.

Winn, Marie. *The Plug-In Drug: Television, Computers, and Family Life.* Penguin. New York: 2002.

An excellent study of the influence of television on children and family life.

Zimmerman, Dimitri A. and Frederick J. Christakis. *The Elephant in the Living Room: Make Television Work for Your Kids.* Rodale Books. New York: 2006.

A positive approach, this book gives scientific evidence that television can be effective tool not just for entertainment, but for education and for socialization.

More Information: Websites

www.parentstv.org

A grassroots movement from the Parents Television Council to work with producers, broadcasters, networks, and sponsors to reduce negative and harmful messages to children.

www.ptvn.org

Website of the Parents Television Network with video programs to help with child raising practices.

www.tvguidelines.org

TV Parental Guidelines to help parents and grandparents evaluate television programs for appropriateness for a child's age group.

www.controlyourtv.org

A cable industry website to help understand parental control settings on TVs and remote controls.

BIRD WATCHING

Fun Fact

Birds have to eat half their body weight every day in order to survive.

You won't need an expensive set of binoculars, but having some way to increase magnification can definitely help with those long-distance sightings. If you're not familiar with what kind of birds there are in your part of the country, pick up a handbook that describes them, preferably in full color. You might be amused to see your grandkids thumbing through the book and reading instead of peering out the car windows. We suggest packing a notebook so you can mark down colors of feathers, beaks, and specifics markings (such as white around the eyes). These specifics will allow you to take your sightings home (or to a library) to check online and find out what you and the grandkids saw. Keep a logbook of your sightings, and challenge your grandkids to find as many as they can.

A GRANDPARENTING ASIDE

For us, grandchildren provide a wealth of topics for conversation, as varied as life itself. Some topics, such as death, are not easy to talk about for many people. Keep in mind, though, that kids are more savvy these days, having seen the topic of death come up (probably too often) in the movies they've seen. In *Star Wars,* for example, death is a recurring theme, especially as it relates to Obi-Wan Kenobi. We don't make it a point to bring up the topic of death, but we do seize opportunities as they present themselves. For example, we've talked about how the spiritual afterlife is presented in *Star Wars.* It's good to remember, though, that grandchildren can be emotional, so be prepared to talk about life and death and to be gentle with your approach.

WHILE YOU'RE BIRD WATCHING:

▶ What is the Audubon Society? (It's an organization dedicated to preserving and restoring natural ecosytems, focusing on birds, other wildlife, and their habitats.)

▶ What are the closest living descendents of dinosaurs? (birds)

▶ What kind of bird would your grandchild like to be? A large, powerful eagle? A darting hummingbird? How about a penguin? (not that you'll find any of these from your car)

▶ Keep a notebook log of the new birds you see. Include bird descriptions, dates and times, etc. We have a friend who has kept a bird-sighting log for over 40 years!

BOUNCY BALL

Did you ever play Two Square in your driveway? What fun! The bouncy balls we used back then were about 12 inches in diameter and bounced very easily (as opposed to a basketball, which required some effort to push down to get it to bounce back up to your hand). Two Square is played just like tennis, except instead of a net, you use a crack in the pavement as the dividing line. You'll bounce the ball into your opponent's square by hitting it with an open palm. If it bounces twice in their square, or your opponent fails to return it to your square, you score a point! The first player to earn 11 points wins. There are dozens of other games you can make up.

▶ Taking turns throwing the ball against a wall. Catch it before it hits the ground to score a point.

▶ Play catch and score a point for a catch, subtracting a point for each drop. Continue for a pre-designated amount of time.

- Throw a ball against a wall, then clap once before catching it. Next time, clap twice. See who can clap the most times between throwing and catching the ball.
- Just buy a bouncy ball and get ready for fun!

A GRANDPARENTING ASIDE

One of the things we noticed that grandchildren seem to have difficulty learning is the concept of records. There's an old joke about something going on "your permanent record." Don't try to scare your grandchildren, but do make sure they know that the grades that they earn in ninth grade are going to be there all the way through their high school career. Eventually they will be factored in to a final GPA (grade point average) which will be looked at by colleges' academic admission panels—not to mention scholarship committees! There are other kinds of records that stay around, too. Traffic tickets will raise auto insurance rates, and will stay on the record for years. So, tell your grandchildren about records and let them know that some of their actions will affect their lives for years to come.

WHILE YOU'RE PLAYING BALL:

- Can you throw the ball back and forth 100 times without dropping it?
- Do the grandchildren want to draw any designs on the ball?
- Can anybody balance the ball on a finger?
- How about on their heads?
- If you're right-handed, try throwing with your left hand (and vice versa).

READING

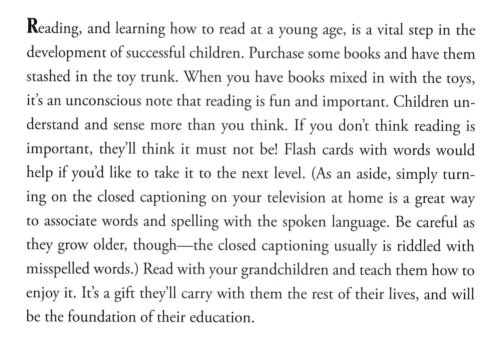

Fun Fact

Albert Einstein didn't talk until he was four years old or read until he was nine.

Reading, and learning how to read at a young age, is a vital step in the development of successful children. Purchase some books and have them stashed in the toy trunk. When you have books mixed in with the toys, it's an unconscious note that reading is fun and important. Children understand and sense more than you think. If you don't think reading is important, they'll think it must not be! Flash cards with words would help if you'd like to take it to the next level. (As an aside, simply turning on the closed captioning on your television at home is a great way to associate words and spelling with the spoken language. Be careful as they grow older, though—the closed captioning usually is riddled with misspelled words.) Read with your grandchildren and teach them how to enjoy it. It's a gift they'll carry with them the rest of their lives, and will be the foundation of their education.

A GRANDPARENT ASIDE

Become an "instant expert" on a subject you know your grandkids are interested in. (For example, dinosaurs. A quick search online will tell you the basic types, and you can thrill your grandchildren by telling them facts about these long-lost creatures.) Don't tell them that you just looked up all of those facts a few minutes before they arrived. Savvy kids will know the instant nature of your being an expert, but that's okay. It will encourage them to learn things. The more fun you can make learning, the more the grandkids will learn. Becoming an "instant expert" is a great way to teach them how much fun it can really be. A great example is the fun facts in this book. If you have a dozen fun facts about dinosaurs, you'll be an entertainment guru! And they'll be learning while they're being entertained.

WHILE YOU'RE TEACHING THEM TO READ:

▶ How did you learn to read? Was it later in life than they're learning? Earlier?

▶ What are some advantages of learning how to read well? (Doing well in school, getting good grades, and a good job. It can also save time on those pesky instructions for those build-at-home furniture kits!)

▶ Encourage them to be the first kid on the block at their age to learn how to read!

▶ At breakfast, find words that the grandchildren know on cereal boxes and go over the spelling.

HARMONICA

A great beginner instrument for an introduction to music is a harmonica. It doesn't have to be an expensive one, although the really cheap ones may sound a bit unpleasant. Still, a Hohner harmonica for beginners won't break the bank. You can find notes for simple songs like *Old Mac-Donald* online and print out the notes, allowing you to learn the song at your leisure later. The idea here is not to become very proficient, just to provide an introduction to the idea of playing an instrument. If the grandchildren love it and want to continue learning on their own, that's great! Harmonicas are a great way to get started in the musical realm. You can try other instruments as well, such as a recorder, a toy piano, or a xylophone. Our personal favorite was the glockenspiel!

A GRANDPARENT ASIDE

We believe that one of the greatest attributes that grandparents bring to the table is their perspective. Grandparents aren't out to impress their peers the way that teenagers are, have lived long enough to know what the long-term effects of certain lifestyles are, and understand the effects that decisions made early on will have later in life. So, how do you make this work for you? Just remember that facts can be more convincing than emotional arguments. While emotional appeals can sway decisions, your honest advice will win the race. Keep this in mind when the parents are pushing their children too hard. You can point to successful people who have ended up unhappy, not well-rounded. On the other hand, if the parents have a don't-care attitude, this could affect the grandkids just as much. Describe the effects of that on a child, based on your lifelong observations.

WHILE YOU'RE PLAYING A HARMONICA OR OTHER MUSICAL INSTRUMENT:

▶ Why did cowboys like harmonicas? (They easily fit in pockets.)

▶ Would they like their own harmonica?

▶ See if the grandchildren can play with a steady beat. (Much easier with an instrument like a drum!)

▶ How fast can you play a series of wild notes? Make it into a contest!

▶ Can they demonstrate the highest and lowest notes on their musical instrument?

▶ How long can everybody play a single note?

HULA HOOP

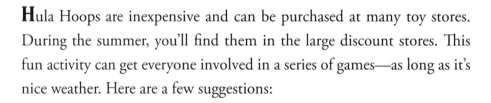

Fun Fact

Hula Hoops were introduced in 1958, and over 20 million were sold within the first six months.

Hula Hoops are inexpensive and can be purchased at many toy stores. During the summer, you'll find them in the large discount stores. This fun activity can get everyone involved in a series of games—as long as it's nice weather. Here are a few suggestions:

- ▶ See how many times everybody can twirl the hoop around his or her waist.
- ▶ Who can keep it going the longest?
- ▶ Instead of rolling a Hula Hoop forward like a tire, pitch it forward and put backward spin on it like the back spin on a cue ball. The spin on the Hula Hoop will overcome the forward motion and return to you if your aim is true.
- ▶ Play catch with Hula Hoops (this isn't easy!).
- ▶ Hold the Hula Hoop while the grandchildren making tumbling acrobatic moves through it.

Kids will figure out different ways to play with their Hula Hoops, and usually all you have to do is stand back and watch the fun. If you need some exercise or want to have fun yourself, join in!

A GRANDPARENTING ASIDE

While it's really important to keep a healthy relationship with your grandchildren, it's just as important to maintain healthy relationships with your adult children and their spouses. This can be especially true if anybody is involved in a divorce, past or present. Stay out of domestic squabbles. They are adults and they have to work things out for themselves. Your concern at this point should be the grandchildren—so of course you'll want to have a civil relationship with both of their parents. We've had friends whose squabbles lasted years, and the end result was the grandparents missing years of their grandchildren's lives. So, do whatever it takes, whether it's swallowing your pride or biting your tongue, to keep the relationship with your children open. It's so you can continue to have those close relationships with your grandchildren.

WHILE YOU'RE PLAYING
WITH A HULA HOOP:

▶ Why isn't there a Hula Square? (If they don't get it, share the joke.)

▶ Have everybody guess the diameter of a hoop, then when you get home, take a measurement and see who's closest to being right.

▶ How high can they throw a Hula Hoop?

▶ Ask if they know where hula dancing originated. (Hawaii)

STORYTELLING

> ## Fun Fact
>
> The National Council of Teachers of English includes the use of "gestures" in its definition of storytelling.

Storytelling is becoming a lost art. You can do your part to keep this activity alive by sitting down with your grandchildren and telling them about the good ol' days. You don't need to go on hour after hour with your entire life, however. It might not hold their interest. But telling them a story about a particular event in your life can be a great way to teach them how to tell stories—it's teaching a skill by example. And remember, if you don't tell your grandchildren about some of the stories of your lives, how will they understand what life was like before their era? What a great way to pass on information! After you tell your story, you can have a discussion about why certain points in the story were relevant. Talk about how the story ended. Have your grandchildren tell you a story about something that happened to them, and explain the difference between recounting events and telling a story. (The story makes the events more dramatic.) If you want to see the pros at work, there are many storytelling festivals that can found on the Internet. (Try looking at www. loc.gov/loc/cfbook/bookfair.html.)

A GRANDPARENT ASIDE

Kids are fascinated by weather. Nearly everybody has a story to tell that's weather related. Do you remember that 10-foot snowfall that you got caught in when you were 20 years old? Tell your grandchildren about it. You can talk to them about the weather that's the norm in other parts of the country. If you live in a hilly region, tell them about the flatlands. If you're in the desert, talk about the ocean. Our son's friend from Texas visited the north during a snowstorm. He was a U.S. Marine and 23 years old and yet he still spent hours playing in the Michigan snow, unashamedly making angels and snowmen and forts with the preschoolers. An aside to the wise: Make sure they are clearly hearing what you are saying when you describe things. See our son's tornado/tomato story on page 82.

WHILE YOU'RE STORYTELLING:

▶ Can your grandchildren tell you a story? (no matter how brief)

▶ What is a "tall tale?" (an exaggerated story like Paul Bunyon and Pecos Bill)

▶ What's the most interesting story they've heard in school or from a friend?

▶ Show them how to use hand movements to make dramatic points (like banging your fist emphatically on the armrest of the car seat).

CROSSWORD PUZZLES

Fun Fact

The New York Times first published their Sunday crossword puzzle in 1942 and their daily puzzle in 1950.

Pack some activity and puzzle books for all ages for use in the car. Make sure you have pencils, too—and a pencil sharpener! If your grandkids are older, you can have them help you with adult puzzles instead of working on the juvenile ones. This fun activity might take some getting used to, but will definitely teach a larger vocabulary and exercise their brains. How many times have they struggled to find that word "on the tip of their tongue"? Try to make this activity a habit, say once a month. If they resist, just go for a couple of times a year. In the end, everybody will win, especially when they score high on the written segment of their college entrance exams! When you first start to play, peek at a few of the answers to make sure the grandkids understand the subtleties of the puzzles. Use a pencil so you can erase mistakes. Cut out successfully filled-out puzzles and put them on the refrigerator so everyone can see the great work!

A GRANDPARENT ASIDE

It doesn't cost much to send lightweight packages via the U.S. Postal Service. If you're on a budget, look into the options available from your post office and you'll be pleasantly surprised. Often, grandparents live in a different part of the country and some things are available there that aren't where the grandchildren live. For example, the grandparent who lives in Florida and the grandkids who live in Kansas. Why not send them some beach memorabilia? There all kinds of knickknacks that you can find at beach shops. One of our favorites is a turtle constructed out of small seashells. You could also visit a bargain store or a Goodwill store and find an inexpensive gift. What about an antique store? Take your time, search around, and buy that "perfect" gift. If you talked to your grandchildren last week and your granddaughter mentioned starting to play in a T-ball league, find a baseball cap! It's a great way to bond with your grandchildren, even if you live far away. You can also do this if you live nearby. Everyone loves getting mail. This is a good way to go straight to your grandchildren, developing a relationship with them while avoiding the middlemen (i.e., the parents).

WHILE YOU'RE WORKING
ON CROSSWORD PUZZLES:

▶ See if they'd like to pick out their own book of puzzles during the next visit to a bookstore.

▶ If you don't know the answer to a clue, say, "How puzzling!"

▶ See if they know what antonyms are. (Antonyms are words pairs that have opposite meanings, such as hot and cold, up and down, etc.)

▶ How many words can they think of that have different meanings but are spelled or pronounced the same? (For example, stalk is a noun and a verb. Too, two, and to are all pronounced the same way.)

▶ What's this called? (a homonym)

10

'TIS THE SEASON

▼

SOME ACTIVITIES, SUCH as playing in snow, are season specific. These kinds of activities are in this chapter, along with activities for specific holidays. If you do not celebrate some of these holidays, such as Easter, just skip over them or adapt them for your own beliefs. Some of the best memories that children have are season specific. We all remember summers at the beach, or jumping in piles of leaves in the fall. So be sure to make those memories with your grandchildren, too.

It's also a good idea to be flexible with your holiday schedule. If you want to have your Easter egg hunt on the weekend before or the weekend after Easter—great! You'll make taking care of the grandkids a lot smoother than it could be. Can you imagine what would happen if all of the parents (who might be divorced) and grandparents wanted the kids over on Easter Sunday? There'd have to be a transporter worthy of the *Star Trek* movies to make that happen. Remember to relax, have fun, and spend time with your grandchildren doing holiday and seasonal activities, whether it's actually on the holiday or not!

DID YOU KNOW?

The American way of raising children has changed greatly in recent decades. For many, a child's self-esteem is paramount. We agree that care must be given to ensure that a child's self-esteem is nurtured, but there are cases where this can be taken too far. Games that have winner and loser labels have been removed from school systems because it was decided no child should be called a loser. One of the first games to go was dodge ball. A typical game nowadays has no winners, only players on a stage (such as role-playing games). Remember, there's no award for second place when it comes to winning that promotion at work, getting passing grades in college, or even in the Super Bowl. Instead of going overboard like that, help your grandchildren's self-esteem by giving them plenty of one-on-one time. Don't be afraid to talk to your grandchildren about losing contests. Mention that even Michael Jordon was cut from his high school varsity basketball team. He was probably disappointed, but it sure didn't stop him from trying. It might even have made him try harder.

MORE INFORMATION: BOOKS

Healy, Sherry. *Confident Child: A Tale and Affirmations to Build a Child's Self Esteem.* Writers Club Press. Lincoln, NE: 2002.
This story of adventure is designed to create confidence in your child.
Ireland, Karin. *Boost Your Child's Self-Esteem: Simple, Effective Ways to Build Children's Self-Respect and Confidence.* Berkley Trade. New York: 2000.
Teaches you how to develop a foundation of inner strength in your child.
Pickhardt, Carl E. *Keys to Developing Your Child's Self-Esteem.* Barron's Educational Series. Hauppauge, NY: 2000.
Emphasizes ways to encourage, foster creativity, learn to cope, think positively, and enjoy competition.

Ramsey, Robert D. *501 Ways to Boost Your Child's Self-Esteem.* McGraw-Hill. Columbus, OH: 2002.
Teaches parents how to guide their children to develop positive self-images.

More Information: Websites

www.kidshealth.org
Includes a wide variety of information to improve health, including mental health. Website is divided into different sections for parents/grandparents, kids, and teens.

www.childdevelopmentinfo.com/parenting/self_esteem.shtml
Basic suggestions to help with a child's self-esteem. Provides a good overview of how to approach the subject of self-esteem.

www.more-selfesteem.com/child_self_esteem.htm
Bulleted list of actions to improve a child's self-esteem. Includes a sign-up page for a monthly newsletter.

www.kidsource.com/kidsource/content2/strengthen_children_self.html
More of a scholarly approach to a child's self-esteem. Has good approaches based on different age groups.

EGG HUNT

Fun Fact

In 1878 President Rutherford B. Hayes and his wife Lucy opened the White House grounds to children for egg rolling on Easter Monday. The event has been held on the South Lawn ever since.

Have the grandchildren wait in their rooms while you go around and "hide" the Easter eggs. You can also use candy and other Easter goodies instead of hardboiled eggs. There's an easy way to make this suitable for older kids, but it will require some thinking ahead of time. You're going to need written clues (printed from the computer is fine) on where to find the eggs. For example, write the clue "Where the mail comes," and hide Easter eggs in the mailbox! Scale the clues depending on age. How about "Beneath the aquatic wonderland" for under the aquarium? If you have more than one grandchild, be sure that everybody gets an equal number of turns at reading the clues and that there are enough eggs in each hiding spot.

A GRANDPARENT ASIDE

While we're thinking about food and good nutrition, a subject that we strongly urge you discuss with the grandchildren's parents, it's sometimes helpful to get together with the grandchildren one day with some magazines, scissors, poster board, and tape or glue. Go through the magazines (ones that feature healthy foods would be great), and cut out pictures of food that the grandchildren like. Tape them to the poster board. Title the poster board "My Favorite Foods" or something similar. The trick here is to put healthy foods on the poster board. No soda pop allowed! And if they can't remember if they tried something in particular, such as a tomato, make it a point to buy some. Try eating them the next time the grandchildren are over. They might be amazed at some of the food they like and how healthy it is. Let's not become a deep-fried nation of the abysmally overweight!

WHILE YOU'RE ON AN EASTER EGG HUNT:

► Tell your grandchildren about some of the Easter holidays you remember in your life.

► Do they know that eggs are a symbol of birth and re-birth (Easter)?

► Do they know how to hypnotize a chicken? (Lay it on its back and draw an X in the dirt beside one of its eyes.)

► Make sure everybody eats an egg. If they don't like eggs, suggest something equally healthy instead.

PLANTING

Fun Fact

Nearly 20 million people planted a Victory Garden during WWII, supplying the nation with over 40 percent of its vegetables.

Before deciding to get ambitious and plant an entire garden, consider how much upkeep this may take. Other options may include an herb garden, but if you're already interested in gardening, you can get your grandchildren to help you with yours. You can find small planters at nearly every large store. Check out the gardening section and take your grandchildren to look at the seed packets. Let them pick out (with guidance!) what they want to plant. Check the seed packets for sunlight requirements and make sure your grandchildren understand which window or porch (depending on the how much sunlight and/or shade is required) to place the seedlings on once they sprout. Do they want something pretty to look at, such as a flower, or something edible like a cucumber? Make sure that whatever plants you choose will do well in the same area, such as partially shaded or full sun. When you plant the seeds (and we suggest using potting soil and planters), place the planter on a small plate or bowl to catch any extra water that spills out, whether inside on a table or windowsill or outside on a patio, deck, or porch. After the plants have sprouted and are ready for transplanting into a garden, show your grandchildren how to mark the sites of the plantings so that they'll remember what's planted. Finally, go over basic garden care. Grandchildren might not realize that it's possible to overwater some plants, which can kill them.

A GRANDPARENT ASIDE

There are a lot of books on raising intelligent kids. We can boil this down to a few main points. Have intelligent conversations with your grandchildren. Don't treat them like kids or imply that their opinions don't matter because they are young. Ask questions and be interested in their answers. Prod them to think deeper about the implications of what they're saying. If they think nobody should drive cars because of global warming, ask them how are you supposed to get to work and what will happen to all of the laid-off auto workers? Have a conversation. Your grandchildren will know if you ask questions that they're not going to pull the wool over Grandma's or Grandpa's eyes by making unchallenged statements. They'll have to learn about the subject matter they want to talk about. And they'll learn to think. And isn't that what intelligence is all about?

WHILE YOU'RE PLANTING:

▶ What were your experiences with gardening when you were a child?

▶ Did you ever visit or live on a farm? Have your grandchildren? Would they like to?

▶ Visit some of the gardening and seed company websites online and plot out what kind of garden your grandchildren would plant if they had unlimited resources.

▶ We taught our grandchildren the difference between nouns and verbs using the sentence "Tomorrow I will plant a plant." The first "plant" is an action word, and therefore a verb. The second "plant" is a thing, and therefore a noun.

RIVERS AND BOATS

Fun Fact

The Mississippi River is 2,350 miles long and runs from Lake Itasca in Minnesota to the Gulf of Mexico.

This summertime activity doesn't require being near a creek, river, or lake. Just find a slope in your yard, set the water hose at the top, and let the water flow. If you have a country house and there are some parts of your yard that you don't mind digging around in, take a hand spade and dig a small channel. Better yet, let your grandchildren build one! Make sure you tell them you'll bring them fresh water to drink if they're thirsty. Otherwise they'll be sticking the end of the water hose in their mouths. (Not that we ever did that . . .) Once your river is running, you can use anything to float down your river, even sticks. You can also make great boats out of paper. These might not last long, as they will become water-logged quickly, but you can always make more! If everybody is appropriately dressed, spray everyone with water for an extra cool-down! (Make sure you get wet, too, so they know you're not picking on them.) This can be loads of fun and the water will help cool off the grandkids (you, too, if you're game!).

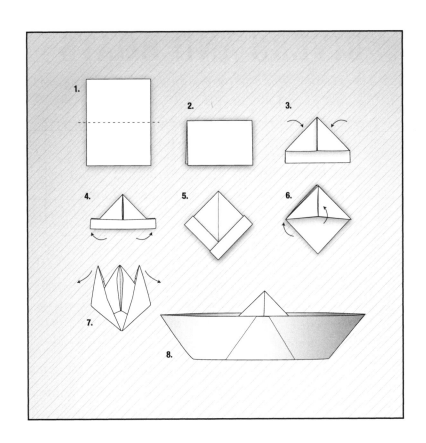

A GRANDPARENTING ASIDE

Younger grandchildren can be finicky eaters. You might worry if they seem to burn zillions of calories and then refuse to eat. One thing that might help is the visual nature of food. Try putting a handful of crackers, baby carrots, cheese squares, and apple slices on a plate. Arrange the food according to color. Then when the grandkids come in, they'll be attracted to the plates and will want to eat. And, of course, this is much healthier than some other options. Keep in mind that water and milk are wonderful drinks for them. Soda and other calorie-filled drinks detract from the meal's nutrition and could send your grandkids down a path leading to obesity. So, keep color in mind when preparing snacks or meals. Show your grandkids how good tasting colorful food can be. Doug's personal favorite is ripe-red tomatoes and deep orange cheese (and blueberries)!

WHILE YOU'RE DIGGING RIVERS:

▶ Ask the grandkids if they know what makes the water run downhill. (gravity)

▶ What would happen if you block the flow of water? What would it be called? (A dam, which would back up the water.)

▶ Does everyone know how to sing "Row, Row, Row Your Boat"?

▶ Get everybody to wiggle their toes in the mud. What does it feels like?

SAND CASTLES

Fun Fact

Glass is made by combining silica sand with burnt lime or limestone and soda ash.

During the summer months, grandchildren are usually out of school and have more free time. This is a perfect chance to engage them in activities, when their hectic schooldays pace is temporarily over. While building sand castles is normally a beach activity, you can make them in a sandbox, too. Before you dive into the creation, talk about your plans. You might decide that everybody will work on the same sand castle, or assign everyone their own castle. One of the younger grandkids might want to team up with you. It doesn't really matter; the object here is to have fun. Will it have a moat? How many towers? Will there be a building inside the outer wall? How about several walls? You can hang a small flag from your castle's wall once it's done. You could even ask your grandchildren to sketch out a few ideas on paper. Who knows—maybe this will create an interest in being an architect. That's the great thing about trying new things. You never know what kind of interest you're going to spark. We like to build our castles close to the water. We know they're temporary, and the next high tide will wipe them out. Part of the fun is to see how long our impregnable castle walls can withstand the onslaught of the mighty seas!

A GRANDPARENTING ASIDE

When you're at the beach, keep a kitchen timer handy at all times. It's great for keeping track of how much sun you and the grandchildren are getting. Nobody likes getting burned! Around the house, a timer can be used for many things. If you're having a discipline problem and are sending a grandchild to the "time-out" room, use a timer to set the length of the sentence. What about brushing teeth? Three minutes of teeth brushing is a good rule of thumb, but you'd be surprised how long it really is. How about when everybody needs to get ready for a trip in the car? You can set the timer for ten minutes and announce that that's when you're heading out the door, ready or not! If their favorite cartoon is coming on in forty-five minutes and you're afraid you'll forget because you're in the middle of an activity (maybe one in this book), use the timer. You can also use it to count down the time to when their parents are coming to pick them up.

WHILE YOU'RE BUILDING SAND CASTLES:

▶ Have the grandchildren seen any castles or forts?

▶ Ask if they'd like to one day see any of the great castles in Europe.

▶ Talk about the castles you have seen.

▶ How difficult must it have been to have fresh water in a castle under siege?

MINI-PARADE

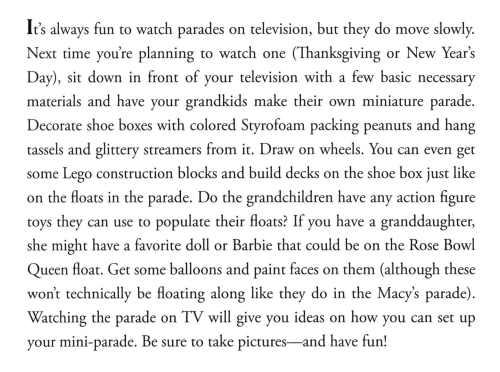

Fun Fact

Newport Beach, California held its first lighted boat parade on July 4, 1908.

It's always fun to watch parades on television, but they do move slowly. Next time you're planning to watch one (Thanksgiving or New Year's Day), sit down in front of your television with a few basic necessary materials and have your grandkids make their own miniature parade. Decorate shoe boxes with colored Styrofoam packing peanuts and hang tassels and glittery streamers from it. Draw on wheels. You can even get some Lego construction blocks and build decks on the shoe box just like on the floats in the parade. Do the grandchildren have any action figure toys they can use to populate their floats? If you have a granddaughter, she might have a favorite doll or Barbie that could be on the Rose Bowl Queen float. Get some balloons and paint faces on them (although these won't technically be floating along like they do in the Macy's parade). Watching the parade on TV will give you ideas on how you can set up your mini-parade. Be sure to take pictures—and have fun!

A GRANDPARENTING ASIDE

So, do you know how your grandchild spends evenings? Doing home-work or taking ballet lessons? Soccer practice or playing in the back yard? It's great to talk about this with your grandchildren and ask them about what kind of choices they're making in how to spend their evenings. Choices in how to spend free time is an area in which grandparents can be especially helpful because they provide a caring perspective that can be somewhat different than the parents have. Parents, after all, have to con-sider how much time and money they have to participate in organized activities. Ask your grandchildren what they think about their choices. Your grandchildren are going to have opinions, even if they don't come right out and express them. Of course, they might not know how to ex-press their feelings. So, talk to them, get a feel what they think is the best way to spend their free time.

WHILE YOU'RE MAKING FLOATS:

▶ Have everybody "rate" each float on TV on a scale from 1 to 10. Explain the rating.

▶ Do they see the peepholes that drivers are using to see as they drive the floats along the parade route?

▶ Count the number of trombones in each band. Does any have 76?

▶ What are their favorite floats in the parade on TV?

HALLOWEEN

Fun Fact

Invented in 1896, Tootsie Rolls were the first wrapped penny candy in America.

Turn your place into a haunted house! There are many ways to create your "haunted" effects. One of our favorites is to make little bobble ghosts. Tie white paper towels around Styrofoam packaging peanuts. Draw eyes around the head and then tie one to each blade of a ceiling fan. Turn the fan on and watch your ghosts fly 'round and 'round. We suggest a low fan speed or else your ghosts might go flying off in all directions. Younger grandchildren can draw monsters or bats. Remember that in their minds, if they can draw a monster, they have control over that monster. It's a method for helping them to gain control over their fears of the unknown. You can use lacy tablecloths for spider webs, then pin your home-made spiders to them. How about taking a large box and making your own haunted house? You could find some Christmas lights (ones that don't get warm or hot) for your haunted house. Paint it and play eerie music. You can find Halloween theme music at most online music stores. Try doing a search online.

A GRANDPARENT ASIDE

If you have your grandchildren on trick-or-treat night, remember to inspect their treats when they get home. They shouldn't eat anything before you've had a look. It's sad but this needs to be done for their safety. You should watch your local newscasts and their websites for what you should be looking for. If you are worried about this, we suggest only taking your grandchildren to households you know in the immediate area. You should also keep this in mind when you're selecting treats to hand out. Individually wrapped candy or treats will help put parents' and grandparents' minds at ease.

WHILE YOU'RE CREATING A HAUNTED HOUSE:

▶ What are your grandchildren afraid of? Don't allow them to say "nothing"—that won't wash. Loosen them up by talking about what you're afraid of, even if it's just heights.

▶ Are they going to any Halloween parties?

▶ Is anybody at school dressing up for Halloween?

▶ Talk like a bad-acting vampire—"I vant to suck your blood, bwah hah hah!"

▶ What scary movie do they want to watch later?

THANKSGIVING COOKING

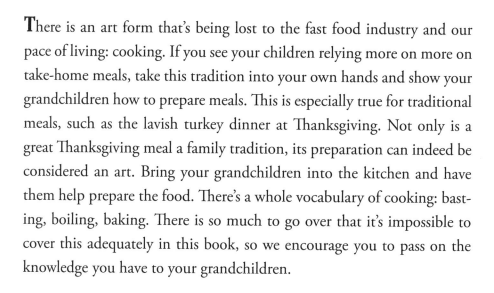

Fun Fact

Benjamin Franklin wanted the national bird to be the turkey, not the eagle.

There is an art form that's being lost to the fast food industry and our pace of living: cooking. If you see your children relying more on more on take-home meals, take this tradition into your own hands and show your grandchildren how to prepare meals. This is especially true for traditional meals, such as the lavish turkey dinner at Thanksgiving. Not only is a great Thanksgiving meal a family tradition, its preparation can indeed be considered an art. Bring your grandchildren into the kitchen and have them help prepare the food. There's a whole vocabulary of cooking: basting, boiling, baking. There is so much to go over that it's impossible to cover this adequately in this book, so we encourage you to pass on the knowledge you have to your grandchildren.

A GRANDPARENT ASIDE

Help teach your grandchildren the rewards of giving. This might sound a bit hypocritical to you, but they might just need an introduction into how much of a joy it is to give gifts. Thanksgiving meals or snacks are a great gift, in this way. Perhaps you can prepare a few take-out desserts and visit your local pediatric ward or nursing home. Call ahead and see if they could use some young visitors to come in and hand out pieces of pumpkin pie! Encourage your grandchildren to give of themselves. Tell them about karma, about how the good deeds that they do will be returned to them someday.

WHILE YOU'RE COOKING:

- ▶ Talk about the different parts of an egg: the yolk, embryo, and shell.
- ▶ Ask them three things they're thankful for this year, and tell them three things you are thankful for.
- ▶ Have everyone give their best impression of a turkey call. *Gobble, gobble, gobble!*
- ▶ Talk about some of the Thanksgiving meals you remember having when you were a child. Share your special memories.
- ▶ Talk about how some Thanksgiving traditions can vary. We know some people of Italian descent who prepare spaghetti for Thanksgiving and homemade ravioli for Christmas.

SNOW

Fun Fact

The word Himalayas means the
"home of snow" in Sanskrit.

Even if you don't live in the north, there are plenty of opportunities to visit people who have snow. And when you do, what grand fun! It seems that even grandkids who have never played in snow know how to build snowmen. Remember to bring along items of clothing to dress your snow people, like sunglasses, hats, and scarves. Bring along some food dye and give your snow people some unique color. You can build little snow people to represent snow grandchildren. Do your grandchildren know how to make snow angels? Teach them if they don't: lie flat on your back in fresh snow and sweep your arms up and down at your sides. Stand up and look at the shape you left on the ground. A snow angel! What about using your sand castle designs to make snow castles? Get creative and make anything you want. How about snow alligators or other kinds of snow animals? Bring the camera along for this activity and be sure everybody is dressed for the weather. Little feet and noses can get very cold very quickly.

A GRANDPARENT ASIDE

This is something that their parents should already be stressing, but it never hurts to reinforce a good lesson. This one is simple. Wash your hands often! It's the one thing your grandkids can do to easily reduce the risks of getting sick. Last year we traveled through an airport. So many people! So many germs! We forgot to wash our hands several times and we all ended up with colds. Make sure your grandchildren are washing their hands often, especially after they come in from outside or after they've been in contact with a lot of other people.

WHILE YOU'RE PLAYING IN THE SNOW:

▶ Is it true that every snowflake is unique? (yes)

▶ How many sides are there to every snowflake? (six, because water crystals are hexagonal)

▶ What is their snowman's name?

▶ What sort of songs do they know about snow? ("Frosty the Snowman," "Let it Snow," etc.)

S
N
O
W

GIFT MAKING

Fun Fact

Many of the sweaters worn by Mr. Rogers on the show "Mr. Rogers' Neighborhood" were knitted by his mother.

Giving can be a tremendous boost to someone else's day. Just imagine the look on Mom's or Dad's face when the grandchildren come home after a visit with their grandparents bearing homemade gifts! When preparing for this exercise, think about some of the gifts you made for your parents. How about:

▶ a frame made out of popsicle sticks with a picture of the grandchild inside
▶ a money dish made of molding clay
▶ the drawing of a big heart with Mom and Dad in it
▶ a can covered with a drawing for a pencil holder
▶ a card or drawing with glitter pens
▶ a wood carving or whittling
▶ a mat decorated with markers or watercolors to frame their school photo

Be sure to mention how you feel when you give somebody a gift. Hopefully you can pass along the sense of the joy of giving to your grandchildren.

A GRANDPARENT ASIDE

A date that's important in many people's lives is their birthday. We suggest having the grandchildren make gifts for others, such as their friends, on their birthdays. When it's the grandchild's birthday, sit down and have a talk with them about its importance. Sure, it's a day where the focus is on them, and they will probably get a lot of gifts, but it's important for other reasons, too. Birthdays are mile markers on their roads to adulthood. Talk to them about the growth you've seen in them in the last year. Tell them how proud you are of their progress. You'll be a great grandparent in their eyes!

WHILE YOU'RE HELPING TO MAKE GIFTS:

▶ Talk about some of the gifts you've given that have brought joy to people.

▶ Talk about some of the gifts you've gotten that have brought you joy.

▶ What's the best gift they ever got?

▶ What gift would they like to get if money was no object?

DECORATIONS

Fun Fact

During the 2006 holiday season,
1.76 billion candy canes were made.

One of our favorite activities beginning a couple of weeks before Christmas is to make chains. These can be made out of many different things, from strips of colored paper to gold or silver foil. Aluminum foil is great, too. Cut half-inch wide strips about three inches long. Tape the strip into a loop to make a link, then loop the next strip through the previous "link" and tape it shut. Loop your next link through the next one. Before you know it, you'll have colorful chains that you can drape across different rooms to make any atmosphere a festive one.

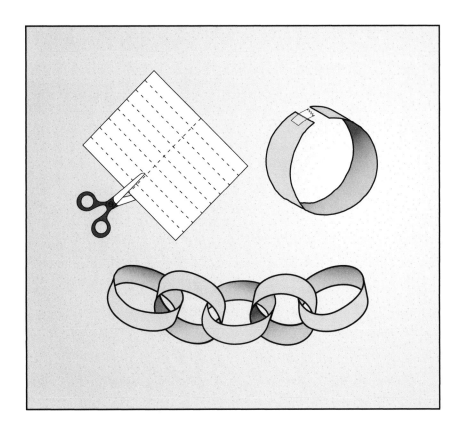

It's good to note that many of the smaller crafts that can be made year-round can be used as tree ornaments. It's fun, too, to have a theme. How about birds? Use your imagination and have fun!

Some suggestions for
other decorations you can make:

▶ Spray paint pine cones and tie strings to them to create a hanging ornament.

▶ Fold paper twice (or more), make cuts with scissors, and unfold for snowflakes.

▶ Maybe you can have all of your grandchildren make small birds by painting thread spools, or gluing together Styrofoam packaging peanuts.

▶ Paint and add some feathers (frayed painted cardboard) to your creations for wings!

A GRANDPARENTING ASIDE

Holidays are important traditions. While their environment may be different than the one you grew up in, it's always good to introduce your grandchildren to the traditions of your youth. As children, Doug's family opened presents on Christmas Eve. Today, we compromise and allow the grandchildren to open just one gift, and they have to wait for Christmas Day for the rest. Keep the traditions of your youth alive, at least by talking about them. Maybe show them some of your past holiday photos. Talk about this, and remind them that those photos will be there when they are grandparents themselves, when you take pictures during the holiday season.

WHILE YOU'RE MAKING
HOLIDAY DECORATIONS:

▶ What do your grandchildren think Christmas (or the holiday of your choice) is all about?

▶ Have they sent any Christmas or holiday cards? If not, why not send one to troops overseas?

▶ Ask them to think about any cool decorations they'd like to make next week or even next year.

▶ What are their favorite decorations?

▶ What do they like most about winter?

11

WHEN YOU'RE RAINED OUT

▼

W

E HAVE ALL had days when plans are washed out. It's easy to blame the weather, then turn on the television and have the grandchildren entertained all day while indoors. Now, there's an option. In this chapter, you'll find a list of activities to refer to when the weather doesn't cooperate and you're rained out. Many of the activities are low cost. Popsicle sticks, for example, can be purchased at many of the larger discount stores or from hobby and craft stores. Plan ahead for when your plans go awry! That way you'll have some of the materials (like Popsicle sticks and a bottle of wood glue) in a drawer for when you're rained out. Then you can save the day by announcing the new plan—one of the activities in this chapter. So dig in, and enjoy the sound of the rain on your roof. It's really quite a lovely sound (and nap-inducing, we must admit).

DID YOU KNOW?

A common teenage trait is expectation of instant gratification. There can be no doubt that American culture today promotes this. Why spend months working off that extra weight when a trip to a doctor for liposuction can have you instantly thin? Why save money and work hard when you can hit the lottery or visit a casino and get rich instantly? Why spend hours preparing a delicious meal when you can just drive to the nearest fast food store to quickly sate your appetite? You should keep this trend in mind when you are taking care of the grandchildren. It's easy enough to say that patience is a virtue and that all good things come to those who wait, but youngsters may need more concrete examples. Tell them stories about how you achieved your goals after long periods of time. Point out that quick fixes are often illusory in nature. (For example, people who got liposuction did get thin, but they will gain all that weight back because they haven't changed their lifestyle to a healthy one.) Sometimes there are no shortcuts to success, and hard work is the only way.

MORE INFORMATION: BOOKS

Brooks, Robert and Sam Goldstein. *Raising a Self-Disciplined Child.* McGraw-Hill. Columbus, OH: 2007.

The objective of this book is to help children learn self-discipline and become responsible for their own actions and choices.

Glenn, Stephen H. and Jane Nelsen. *Raising Self-Reliant Children in a Self-Indulgent World: Seven Building Blocks for Developing Capable Young People.* Three Rivers Press. New York: 2000.

Offers workable ideas for developing a trusting relationship with children, as well as how to implement discipline to help your child become a responsible adult.

Marshall, Marvin L. *Discipline without Stress, Punishments, or Rewards: How Teachers and Parents Promote Responsibility & Learning.* Piper Press. Los Alamitos, CA: 2001

This book has great suggestions that show how to encourage positive thinking in school or at home, while giving children the power to choose and self-reflect.

Rosemond, John. *The New Six-Point Plan for Raising Happy, Healthy Children.* Andrews McMeel Publishing. Riverside, NJ: 2006.

Written with both common sense and a sense of humor, this book is great for families feeling overwhelmed by parenting advice.

MORE INFORMATION: WEBSITES

www.azcentral.com/families/articles/0725fam_indulge.html

An excellent article that explains how and why self-indulgence and instant gratification work against a child's best interest.

www.abc.net.au/rn/science/ockham/stories/s599369.htm

Transcript of a radio interview with Margot Prior, a psychology professor, with information about how resilience in children is affected by the culture of instant gratification.

seattletimes.nwsource.com/html/parenting/2003852323_faull25.html

A newspaper column by Jan Faull, a specialist in child development and behavior, about the virtues and benefits of teaching patience to a child.

www.familyeducation.com/

Information runs across a broad spectrum of education topics. Information is broken down by age groups.

POPSICLE STICKS

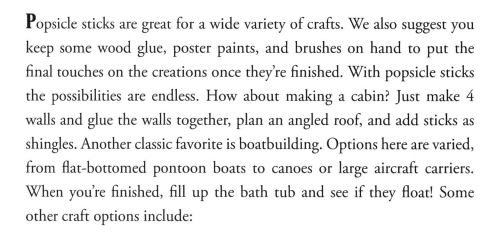

Fun Fact

In 1905, the Popsicle was invented by eleven-year-old Frank Epperson. Later he patented it as the Eppersickle, a name his children changed to "Pop-sicle."

Popsicle sticks are great for a wide variety of crafts. We also suggest you keep some wood glue, poster paints, and brushes on hand to put the final touches on the creations once they're finished. With popsicle sticks the possibilities are endless. How about making a cabin? Just make 4 walls and glue the walls together, plan an angled roof, and add sticks as shingles. Another classic favorite is boatbuilding. Options here are varied, from flat-bottomed pontoon boats to canoes or large aircraft carriers. When you're finished, fill up the bath tub and see if they float! Some other craft options include:

- ▶ Picture frames
- ▶ Coin boxes or piggy-banks
- ▶ Bridges (How about holding a contest to see which bridge will hold the most weight? Use paper clips or pennies as the method of measurement).

Ask your grandkids to use their imaginations; they will find that the possibilities are endless!

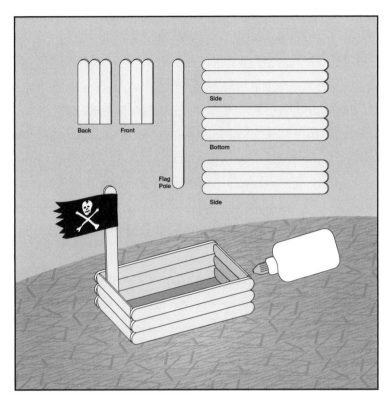

To make a Popsicle stick boat:

1. Glue three Popsicle sticks together for the sides and bottom of the boat.
2. Cut three Popsicle sticks in half and glue the halves together for the front and back of the boat.
3. Assemble and glue together the sides, bottom, front, and back of the boat.
4. Glue your flag on your flagpole, and your flagpole in a corner of the boat.

A GRANDPARENTING ASIDE

From time to time it's a great idea to walk your grandchildren through your home, talk about some of the things you have there and why these things deserve the grandchildren's respect. For example, many people have photographs hanging on a wall. Have you ever told the grandchildren who's in those pictures? You can help establish a sense of family and respect by talking about them. If you have knickknack shelves, you can talk about the items there, why they have meaning to you, where you got them. You can even go through cluttered drawers and closets and talk about some of the items that might be stashed away there. How about things like paintings or other decorations on your walls? Explain why you selected those items and what they mean to you—why they're important. Maybe you got a piece of furniture from some distant land that is interesting to talk about. We often take our homes for granted, and even though our grandchildren have visited us often, we forget that we haven't talked to them about what's important to us, what we've selected to adorn our space. So take a few minutes and give your grandchildren a grand tour of your home to teach them why they should respect the contents in it.

WHILE YOU'RE MAKING POPSICLE-STICK CONSTRUCTIONS:

- ▶ Do they know the proper names of construction materials? (bricks, steel beams, drywall board, etc.)
- ▶ Share stories about any construction jobs you might have had, or someone you know has had.
- ▶ Can they figure out how I-beams got their name? (A cutaway side view looks like the capital letter "I.")
- ▶ Talk about what it feels like to successfully build something from scratch. Do they have a sense of accomplishment?

MYSTERY BOX

This great activity will help your grandchildren develop their sense of touch and encourage their imagination's development. And it's great fun, too! It does require some prep work. Just take a box, such a shoe box, and cut a hand-size hole in the lid. Place a mystery object in the box and have your grandchildren feel the object with their hands, making sure not to look, and try to guess what it is. Start with a simple object, like a shoe or an apple. Can your grandchildren guess a pear from its shape? Move on to harder objects, such as a screwdriver. It's important to make sure that the objects are safe before you select them. A pencil sharpener might seem safe, but little fingers can access those sharp edges. Make sure everybody gets a turn—including you! Have your grandchildren pick out an object (make sure this is a supervised selection; have your spouse double-check for safety reasons), then you try to guess its identity.

A GRANDPARENTING ASIDE

Talk to your grandchildren about their five senses. Many people take "seeing" for granted, but the same can be said of the other senses. How horrible would it be not to hear the warning blare of an approaching train? There are warning sirens that rely on hearing for many things. Do they know that some people who are blind have other senses that are heightened? Have them close their eyes and get around the house by sense of touch. (Follow them to make sure they don't trip over anything or touch something dangerous.) At some street intersections, there are chirping sounds to help let blind people know the state of the traffic light. Hearing isn't the only sense that is heightened. What about the sense of smell? Walk around a flowering garden and have the grandkids take in the scents. Often the first sign that something is on fire is smell, and this alerts us to potential danger. Can they name the five senses? Have them try! Then see if they know what extrasensory perception means, and if they don't, explain it (or have them research it).

WHILE YOU'RE GUESSING THE CONTENTS OF A BOX:

► Talk about trust. It's special that you and your grandchildren can play this game without fear that someone will put something scary in the box.

► Draw a parallel between finding your way ahead in life and identifying the object in a box.

► Do they know the story of Pandora's box? (If you don't know it, have your grandchildren find out and report back to you!)

► Can they name some things that are important about smell and hearing? (Smelling smoke from a dangerous fire or hearing the warning honks from an approaching car.)

M
Y
S
T
E
R
Y

B
O
X

JOURNAL WRITING

Keep notebooks around that are only for your grandchildren to write in. Have a separate notebook for each grandchild. These are their journals, in which they can describe their visits with you. Make sure you don't make this into a chore; it should be fun. Set aside five minutes here and five minutes there for your grandchildren to write their journal entries. They might resist at first or claim to have no idea about what to write. If that's the case, start asking questions:

- ▶ What did you do today?
- ▶ What do you like most about your best friend?
- ▶ What's your favorite animal and why?

When they start to answer, tell them to write it down. This journal will be great for them to look at later in life, and it will also help their writing skills. Penmanship is quickly getting lost in the age of keyboards and spellcheckers. When they're writing essays to get into the college of their choice, give yourself a pat on your back.

A GRANDPARENT ASIDE

Safety always comes first. Today's parents seem to be better at keeping things out of a child's reach. When we were growing up, we knew not to touch things in certain drawers or cabinets. This might be a side effect of the changing role of parenting. In any event, before the grandkids come over, take a few minutes to look around and make sure dangerous and poisonous substances are safely out of reach. Look up poisonous plants that grow in your area and scan your house and yard for any culprits. Kids eat the darnedest things, and if you doubt that, ask Robin about the time her three-year-old claimed (with tears pouring out of his eyes while he scrubbed his tongue with a mittened hand) that he had tasted a dead mouse!

WHILE THEY ARE WRITING
IN THEIR JOURNALS:

▶ Start up your own journal and describe your grandkids' visits. Read it to your grandchildren. Read it right away if they're having trouble getting started writing entries. Wait a year or two to get a great walk down memory lane.

▶ Have your grandchildren ask you to spell any word they're not sure about.

▶ Has anybody learned any new words lately?

▶ Solicit promises not to read each others' journals (that is, if they don't want them read).

GAME DESIGN

It's easy to get out a board game or a deck of cards and play. That's fun and a great activity. But let's take it a step further; have your grandkids ever designed and played their own game? Think about all of those creative energies you'll unleash and exercise in your grandchildren! First, pick out if you want to make a card game or a board game. If it's a card game, start by figuring out how many cards you will hand out. Here are some ideas:

▶ A matching game, in which players must find matches of their suit or their card value. For example, lay out all of the cards face down on a table. Pick a card, then another. If they match, you get the cards and go again. If not, they get turned back over.

▶ Hand out an equal number of cards to everybody playing. Take turns trying to throw a card into a hat (or bowl) a short distance away. Whoever gets the most cards in the hat wins!

▶ Deal out all cards face down in front of the players. Everybody takes turns taking one card from their pile and placing it face up in the center of the table. Whenever a jack is placed faced up, the first person to slap the pile gets all the cards. The winner is the player with the most cards.

▶ For board games, just get a pair of six-sided dice and a piece of cardboard. Draw a trail of squares across the cardboard, curving them all around. You could also draw a spiral, leading to victory in the center. Then draw hazards on the board for fun, like THE DARK FOREST and BOGGY SWAMP. On some of the squares you can write "move back 3 spaces" or "move ahead 2 spaces." Have fun and be creative. The first person to the end square wins! (Hint: you'll need to decide in advance whether or not a person needs an exact roll to end on the final square.)

A GRANDPARENT ASIDE

What do you do when you feel your children are making mistakes in the way they are raising your grandchildren? There's no easy answer to this loaded question. It's a situation where a person is "damned if you do, damned if you don't." Keep a few things in mind: the parents are the ones responsible for raising the kids. It's their responsibility, therefore the decisions are theirs. With that said, you will always have some sort of influence on the decisions they make. The trick is in approaching the situation. Don't make emotional arguments; instead, focus on using logic and reason. If you feel they're pushing the kids too hard with nightly dance, music, ballet, or sports, find data that supports your claim that children are overscheduled. Then, reach a compromise. Suggest giving the kids one night off when they can just be . . . well, kids! And of course, spend

GAME DESIGN

the time you have with the grandkids however you want. You are an influence on their lives. If the grandkids are having their own problems with the parents, talk about the problems you had with your parents. It will help them understand that they aren't alone with their problems.

WHILE YOU'RE DESIGNING A CARD OR BOARD GAME:

▶ What's their favorite card or board game?

▶ What were some of the games you played when you were their age?

▶ Give them an assignment to design another game at their home and then bring it the next time they visit.

▶ Do they have any friends they would like to play the newly designed game with? (This is a good way to get names of their friends.)

ANIMAL SHELTER

Fun Fact

The dog Benji's real name was Higgins. He was "discovered" in an animal shelter in Burbank, California.

When we visited our local animal shelter, we were surprised by the amount of support it received in the forty-five minutes we were present. People donated dog food, toys, and other items that the shelter needed. Most animal shelters are running at full capacity in part because of the lack of education for spaying and neutering our loving pets. We're not suggesting you go to the shelter to look for a new pet, although that could certainly be one of your aims; instead, we suggest you visit just to educate your grandchildren about the number of animals that have no owners. If they're old enough, you might want to explain what happens if nobody adopts an animal. This can be stressful, though, so be careful. Call ahead and see if there are any items the shelter especially needs, then take your grandchildren to the shelter and bring those items.

A GRANDPARENT ASIDE

From time to time, remind yourself to slow down. Not just your pace, but your state of mind. Take a lesson from your grandchildren. A crack in the sidewalk can be endlessly studied by a child: is that a blade of grass or a weed? How does it live between slabs of concrete? Is there a tiny ant hill? How do the ants not get stepped on? Children are absorbed by the little things in life, because everything is fresh and new to them. Take some time to renew your own inner child while you answer their endless questions. You just might find that spending time with your grandchildren and picking up some of their unbridled curiosity will make you feel younger.

WHILE YOU'RE AT AN ANIMAL SHELTER:

▶ Watch other people as they pick out animals they want to adopt. Ask your grandkids if they know the reasons behind the selection.

▶ See how many breeds of dogs and cats your grandkids know. Tell them how many you know.

▶ Most shelters have an area in which you can visit with a dog. Take one out and have a good talk with the dog.

▶ Pick up any brochures they have and read them to your grandchildren.

FAMILY LETTER

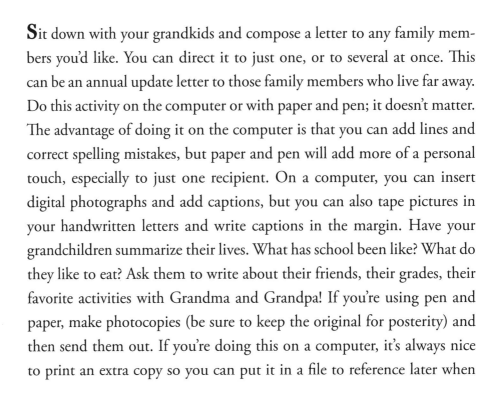

Fun Fact

The United States Post office introduced the Zone Improvement Plan (ZIP codes) in 1963.

Sit down with your grandkids and compose a letter to any family members you'd like. You can direct it to just one, or to several at once. This can be an annual update letter to those family members who live far away. Do this activity on the computer or with paper and pen; it doesn't matter. The advantage of doing it on the computer is that you can add lines and correct spelling mistakes, but paper and pen will add more of a personal touch, especially to just one recipient. On a computer, you can insert digital photographs and add captions, but you can also tape pictures in your handwritten letters and write captions in the margin. Have your grandchildren summarize their lives. What has school been like? What do they like to eat? Ask them to write about their friends, their grades, their favorite activities with Grandma and Grandpa! If you're using pen and paper, make photocopies (be sure to keep the original for posterity) and then send them out. If you're doing this on a computer, it's always nice to print an extra copy so you can put it in a file to reference later when you're doing the next letter. You might be wondering what you wrote in the previous update letter, so have it handy.

A GRANDPARENT ASIDE

It can be tough to answer all of the grandkid's questions. We're supposed to be the wise ones; the people *their* parents go to for advice. So what happens when they ask something you aren't prepared to answer? It's okay to say you don't know the answer. You can say that some people believe one thing and other people believe something else. Then shrug and say, "Hell if I know who's right." Okay, without the cursing! You get the idea. It's good for your grandchildren to know that we're all human and have limits to our knowledge. And although we might certainly have an opinion about everything, sometimes certainty is a difficult thing to come by.

WHILE YOU'RE COMPOSING
A FAMILY LETTER:

▶ What was the last letter they received? (Other than a birthday or holiday card)

▶ What sort of correspondence have you sent and received throughout your life?

▶ Talk about how excited family members will be to get the letter and how much it will mean to them.

DRESS-UP

Most grandchildren have watched more than their share of television. So how can you use this as a springboard? Have them think of some of the roles they've seen in shows, then go to a resale store, such as Goodwill, pick out some clothes, and play dress-up! If the grandchildren are still small, it might be difficult to find a suit and jacket to fit, but there are usually frilly dresses and camouflage clothing. How about flashy shoes? Won't it be fun to have your grandson put on a tie and pretend to be a businessman? There are all kinds of role-playing scenarios to try: kings and queens, superheroes, business people, tea-party goers, athletes. Have fun. See what's available at the resale store, but discuss the roles as you drive there. You'll want to have your camera ready for this activity. And don't forget about your own closets during this activity; you might have plenty of old clothes in a closet that needs cleaning out.

A GRANDPARENT ASIDE

Grandchildren aren't brats, but they can sure act that way sometimes. So what do you do when they're misbehaving? The most important thing is to call attention to their behavior. Sometimes kids act that way to get attention, but other times they want to see what they can get away with. Children always push boundaries, so lay down clear rules for acceptable behavior. If what they're doing is unacceptable, tell them! If they don't adjust, then it's the time-out corner or room for them. Don't get into a battle of words. Make sure the boundary lines are clear, or they will get confused about what's allowed and they'll keep pushing the limits. Talk to the parents about the behavior so that all of the adults are on the same page. We believe that children crave acceptance and praise from the adults in their lives, so use this as a powerful tool to stop and prevent misbehavior. Don't tell their parents all the time; save this for egregious misbehavior so that it achieves its full impact.

WHILE YOU'RE PLAYING DRESS-UP:

▶ Have all the kids come up with cool names for your dressed-up roles, such as Mister or Miss Coolyoungkid or Greatdancer.

▶ Have a meal while everybody is dressed up and continue to play your parts. A tea party is great!

▶ How does their character walk, talk, or move? Try to walk in funny new ways and have everybody use exaggerated arm motions when they speak.

12

GRANDKIDS CHOOSE

▼

SOMETIMES IT'S FUN just to pick an activity at random. Why not let the grandchildren choose? This chapter is full of activities that a grandchild would love to choose from, all of them fun and nurturing, and many educational as well. Not only will you have fun, you'll be bonding with your grandchildren at the same time. So, sit down with your grandchildren and have them read through all the activities in this chapter. Make it their choice to decide what you'll do that day. Alternatively, write down each activity on a piece of paper and place it in a hat and have your grandchild pick one blind. Also, because these activities are for the grandchildren to choose from, they're perfect for those times when the grandkids come over and they're feeling a little blue, for whatever reason. We can all have off days, right? So the next time that happens, have them look through this chapter and find an activity that looks especially fun. Then get ready for fun!

DID YOU KNOW?

Many researchers are alarmed at is the explosion of young children prescribed antidepressants. We understand that for many children and parents this can very much be a blessing. What we are alarmed at, however, is how much we don't know about the potential side effects. Many studies have indicated that antidepressants can cause suicidal tendencies in preteens and teenagers. Keep this in mind if the parents of your grandchild are considering this as an option. Make sure they talk to the doctor about the side effects. And most definitely keep your eyes open for withdrawn behaviors from your grandchildren. It can be a warning sign that they're having emotional problems.

MORE INFORMATION: BOOKS

Abela, John R.Z., and Benjamin L. Hankin. *Handbook of Depression in Children and Adolescents.* The Guilford Press. NY: 2007.

While rather technical, this book gives great examples of vulnerability a n d treatment of child and adolescent depression.

Hockey, Kathleen P. *Raising Depression-Free Children: A Parent's Guide to Prevention and Early Intervention.* Hazelden Publishing & Educational Services. Center City, MN: 2004.

This book has the latest information about childhood depression, as well as practical, everyday advice to reduce your child's risk of developing this life-threatening disease.

Riley, Douglas A. *Depressed Child: A Parent's Guide for Rescuing Kids.* Taylor Trade Publishing. Lanham MD: 2001.

This book explains how to identify the symptoms of depression and also provides tools for treatment decisions

MORE INFORMATION: WEBSITES

www.upliftprogram.com/depression_stats.html

Full of statistics about children and depression. Includes book reviews and a free newsletter.

www.surgeongeneral.gov/library/mentalhealth/chapter3/sec5.html

A United States Surgeon General report about depression and suicide in children and adolescents.

www.keepkidshealthy.com/welcome/conditions/depression.html

Useful advice from a pediatric viewpoint about depression. Includes advice on what to look for in children who might suffer from depression.

ATHLETIC EVENT

Fun Fact

Michael Jordan was cut from the high school varsity team as a sophomore.

Attend an athletic event, such as a basketball game, and record the game statistics for a particular player. Come up with your own form to record the statistics—a stat sheet. The sheet will vary, of course, depending on the sport. For example, in basketball you could record the number of shot attempts and makes, the number of rebounds, and the number of points. For baseball, the number of catches, hits, at-bats, and runs. You get the idea. By the way, this is another great time to use some of that great math ability that you've developed in the activity regarding teaching math, because statistics are numbers, too! Your grandchildren will appreciate not only the time that you've spent attending a sporting event with them, they'll love the fact that you've gone through the effort of helping them record a player's efforts in statistical form! After the contest, go over the stats with them. This is a great activity to help with math skills, and it's a great way to bond.

A GRANDPARENTING ASIDE

As a grandparent, you hold a special place in your grandchildren's lives. After all, you're the one that their parents go to for advice. One of the ways to take advantage of this is when you're talking to your grandchildren about their performance in an athletic contest. You job is to help them realize their potential, but nagging them will not help. Constant praise, even for mistakes, won't help either. Be honest about their performance and always point out the good things that happened. Many children seem to blame themselves for everything with "Oh, woe is me!" zest. If you can give them helpful advice, like their feet need to move more, or that they need to pass more (or less), or that there was an opportunity missed because they didn't realize how much time was left in the game, this could really help their progress without turning them off entirely. Keep a notepad by you during the game to make those notes. We've noticed many things during games that we later forgot.

WHILE YOU'RE RECORDING STATISTICS (AND GOING OVER THEM):

▶ Write cool things in the margins like "Nice shot in the second quarter!"

▶ Ask your grandchild which stat the player needs to improve and what the player should do during practices in order to see improvement.

▶ Although the object of the game is to win, make sure they understand that it is just a game.

▶ Stress how important improvement can be. An average player can be a great player by the end of the season.

▶ See if your grandchild wants to record statistics for the entire team.

SLINGSHOT

This will require a stroll in the woods to locate V-shaped branches that are both small and sturdy. You'll also need a few thick rubber bands. Once you've collected your sticks, you should cut the branch below the V so that you end up with a Y-shaped branch. (If the kids are old enough, have them do this part themselves.) You'll attach a rubber band to each of the tops of the Y. Then cut a small strip of cloth, an inch by three inches, and tie the rubber bands to it. The cloth is the cradle in which you'll load your shots. We suggest using wads of paper instead of hard objects, so young grandchildren especially won't be injured by a misfire. Once everybody has their slingshot, set out your targets someplace where errant shots won't hurt anyone (or damage property). Empty 2-liter soda pop plastic bottles work well. Don't worry too much about getting far away from the target. Kids will be thrilled to hit it even if they're only a few steps away. Compliment all of the participants on their marksmanship! Always stress safety! Never aim a slingshot at anybody—even if it's not loaded. The same goes for any weapon!

A GRANDPARENTING ASIDE

There is a saying that some grandchildren hear all the time: "You'll understand when you're older." Now, while this statement is of course completely true, think about how this might be translated by a grandchild. They might be hearing that they're too immature and aren't smart enough to understand the answer. We suggest saying something else entirely. Why not ask for more time coming up with an answer (don't mention it might take years)? Yes, this puts the onus on you, but you're old enough to be able to handle it, right? So, the next time you think about saying, "You'll understand when you're older," picture it as sounding to the kids as "You're too dumb to understand" and try to come up with an alternate answer to their questions.

WHILE YOU'RE FIRING AT TARGETS:

▶ Do they know the story of David and Goliath? If they don't, tell them. If they do, have them tell it to you.

▶ Wonder aloud if you could survive in the wilderness with only a slingshot to catch your meals.

▶ Would they like a professional slingshot when they get a little older?

▶ See how many "hits" in a row everybody can get.

S
L
I
N
G
S
H
O
T

PHOTOGRAPHS

Fun Fact

About 27,000 photographs
are taken each second.

There's something special about leafing through old photographs. We know many younger people keep their photo albums in a digital format and view them on a computer screen, and while we have some of those, it's the old photographs that are precious—especially the ones dating back to the time before color prints were available. Your grandchildren might not be enthusiastic about this activity (anything without color implies boring for ours), but as they get older they will appreciate their family's history. Go through them first if you have hundreds and hundreds and select the best fifty or so. You'll want to explain each photograph and talk about the person in it. Be sure to look for things in the picture, such as an old bicycle with balloon tires, that can help describe what life was like back when the photograph was taken. If they're old enough and you have extras, pick out a frame or two and give them to your grandchildren as gifts. They might not fully appreciate the gift right away, but they will.

A GRANDPARENT ASIDE

In today's world, where 50% of marriages end in divorce, time can be a big issue when it comes to the grandkids. Their parents might be divorced; you might be divorced; and your adult child's in-laws might be, too. If your parents are alive, one child could have 12 or more sets of grandparents, step-grandparents, and great-grandparents! Keep this in mind and when it comes to scheduling, try to be flexible for your grandchildren's sake. Holidays especially can be stressful; if you're willing to celebrate on a different date you'll find it much more enjoyable than a brief 2-hour visit, because they have to drive to the in-laws, too. Kids are adaptable (you'll get lots of love if you want to celebrate Christmas on the 23rd!), and your adult kids will be endlessly thankful that you've eased their schedule and given them time to relax and enjoy the occasion themselves.

WHILE YOU'RE LOOKING AT OLD PHOTOS:

- ▶ Have everybody select a favorite picture and explain why they picked it.
- ▶ What do your grandchildren think of the hairstyles and clothing styles in the photos? How have these changed over the years?
- ▶ Why do some pictures have special meaning for you?
- ▶ Do your grandchildren have any special pictures at their home?
- ▶ Talk about how some cultures used to be fearful of a camera, thinking that a picture captures part of a person's soul.

P
H
O
T
O
G
R
A
P
H
S

TENNIS

Depending on the age of your grandchildren, we suggest starting out with the cheapest rackets you can find. There's no sense spending a lot of money if they are going to outgrow or be uninterested in the game. Look around for tennis courts that are available for general use. Bring water so that nobody gets dehydrated. Use sunscreen if you're concerned about exposure. If you have membership at a YMCA, that's a sure bet, as are some schools and colleges. If all else fails, hit the ball back and forth across your driveway and don't worry about not having a net. See how many times you and your grandchildren can hit the ball back and forth in a row. Make sure they understand that at first you're trying to hit the ball toward each other. In a competition, of course, players will try to hit the ball where the other player can't reach. Talk about this game before you play, because it will generate a lot of excitement. To heighten this, have the equipment lying out where they can see it. When the time comes, have a blast playing tennis!

A GRANDPARENT ASIDE

While you're preparing a sport-related activity, the children of today have an advantage that we didn't when we were growing up: the large variety of television programming available. While we've spoken out against how much time today's children spend in front of the TV, this is one situation where watching a game will offer excellent educational opportunities. For example, you can usually find a tennis match scheduled for television broadcast at nearly any point during the year. So, take the time to sit down with your grandchildren and watch a match before you head out with them and your rackets. This will give them an idea of the way a tennis game is supposed to be played, and it will save you a lot of explanation later. The same goes for many other sports, such as bowling, lacrosse, and baseball. Another advantage to watching a game or two on TV is the strategy discussions from the analysts. Talk over what's said by those experts with your grandchildren.

WHILE YOU'RE PLAYING TENNIS:

▶ How many times can everybody bounce a ball on their tennis racket?

▶ Do they know the scoring rules? Investigate them with the grandchildren (library or online).

▶ Ask if they would like to watch a tennis match with you on TV.

▶ Talk about how much practice everybody thinks a player needs to become a professional.

▶ Ask what they think their friends would say to an invitation to a game of tennis.

FLOWERS

Visit an arboretum or even a colorful flowerbed in a park to sketch flowers in order to identify them later online. Think of yourselves as explorers who have discovered the Galapagos Islands and are identifying new species. You can even "explore" your own garden. We'll wager that you know the names of the flowers there. If you're admiring a neighbor's gardens, make sure you know the names ahead of time so that you can tell your grandchildren. If you go to an arboretum, you could bring a flower identification book that you can borrow from the library. If your grandchildren enjoy drawing pictures, often you can just look at your own yard. Even though dandelions are considered weeds, they are quite colorful! Once you have finished your sketches and identifications, go online and find pictures and descriptions of why these flowers are unique. Note the colors, the number of leaves, the shape of the stems. Find out what makes each flower different. This is a great way to introduce your grandchildren to botany and to green thumbs.

A GRANDPARENT ASIDE

If your grandchildren are like most, they watch television shows—and with those shows, a lot of TV commercials. We've talked about the difference between reality and acting before, and it's important to remember that as the grandkids watch commercials, which are aimed at convincing the viewer that it's the best product. Kids will watch these commercials and believe them. Why would they lie, right? So it's a good idea to watch commercials with your grandchildren and point out some of the things you notice about commercials and give your grandchildren their first lessons in the way consumerism works in this country (i.e., buyer beware!).

WHILE YOU'RE IDENTIFYING FLOWERS:

▶ Do they know anyone whose is named after a flower? (Rose, Iris, etc.)

▶ Do they know the meaning of the phrase, "A rose by any other name smells as sweet." (It means that a rose would still be beautiful, even if it was named something ugly.)

▶ Ask them what their favorite flowers are.

▶ See if they can guess your favorite flower and explain why they think so.

TRACTOR RIDE

Fun Fact

Benjamin Holt invented the tractor in 1900.

Both of us went on hay rides when we were children and remember them fondly. This often happened when we went out past the hay fields to pick pumpkins. If we remember correctly, these sometimes were school-sponsored events. If you hear about your grandchildren having this opportunity, urge them to take advantage of it. On the other hand, it would be a great memory for them if you can arrange a ride yourself! You can do an Internet search for tractor rides or hayrides in your area. Ask around and see if anybody knows of any in your local area. Make sure everybody understands the safety rules before you head out and that nobody has an allergy issue, then get ready for a great trip. Bring a camera and take pictures. The hayrides we went on were at night, adding to their mystique. You might decide that daytime excursions are a better idea, especially for younger grandchildren.

A GRANDPARENT ASIDE

While this aside is especially for grandparents who are primary caregivers, every grandparent needs to be aware of the influence of grandchildren's peers on them. In some cities, this influence can extend to gangs. Even if your grandchildren seem too young to be involved with such nonsense, remember that gangs recruit members young. It's a good idea to keep that dialog open with your grandchildren. This way you'll know who their friends are. Talk about gangs and the influence they have, and the peer pressure they exert. Involvement with gangs can lead to disastrous results, such as drugs and violence—things to avoid! Warn your grandchildren in advance about bad influences and back them up if they have to go against peer pressure. Remember that it's a difficult thing to do.

WHILE YOU'RE ON A TRACTOR RIDE:

▶ Talk to your grandchildren about any rides you went on as a child.

▶ Can they try to estimate how fast you're going?

▶ Talk about how hay acts like "shock absorbers," which all cars have.

▶ Ask if anybody wants to participate in a singalong.

SKIPPING STONES

Fun Fact

An annual stone-skipping tournament is held every year on Mackinac Island in Northern Michigan.

We've all at least attempted to skip stones. It would be great if you could find some information online that describes good skipping techniques and stone selection. Find a pond or a lake (remember that some slow-moving rivers will also work), to take your grandchildren out for some stone-skipping lessons. Once everyone has the hang of it, hold contests for the most skips, the highest skip, and the farthest skip. It's great if you can have each grandchild win at least one of the contests. Note that you can always make up a category, such as best throw by youngest grand-child. That way, everybody comes out of this activity a winner.

A GRANDPARENTING ASIDE

One of the goals of this book is to help grandparents help their grand-children grow up to become successful adults. But sometimes we can forget about some of the non-obvious ways in which children can become successful adults. While staying out of legal trouble and finding honest work that pays good wages are certainly worthy goals, take some time to think about some other attributes that adults have that we would want our grandchildren to have, such as integrity, a giving spirit, a good nature. This good nature might mean that they won't grow up to be CEO in a cutthroat industry, but by being "good people," our grandchildren can be terrific human beings. And isn't that what being successful is all about? Don't forget about those personal attributes like integrity. These are things that nobody can put a price on.

WHILE YOU'RE SKIPPING STONES:

▶ How many lakes and rivers can they name?

▶ Have they ever seen one of the Great Lakes? Have they ever seen a body of water where they couldn't see the far shore? Would they like to?

▶ How far can everybody throw a stone? Don't worry about skipping it.

▶ See how large a splash you can make with a stone.

SCRAPBOOK

Fun Fact

Historians often rely on scrapbooks for personal accounts when researching historical events.

Making a scrapbook is not only great fun, it's an activity with an end result (the scrapbook) that can be revisited again and again. The idea here is to make a scrapbook of what the grandchild's life is like, his or her favorite foods, colors, activities. Then get some old magazines and look for relevant pictures that can be associated with these things. Cut out the pictures and paste them into the scrapbook. For example, you could cut out a picture of a bowl of macaroni and cheese, then draw a big arrow to it and write, JASON'S FAVORITE FOOD. You get the idea. After you're done, you can put the scrapbook away and pull it out years later and go over it with your grandchildren. They'll be amazed by how much they've grown! Or you can pull it out every time there's a significant event in the grandchild's life and add a page with picture, descriptions, newspaper clippings, and other odds and ends about the event. This is an activity that keeps on giving!

A GRANDPARENT ASIDE

Talk to your grandchildren about how active grandparents can be. One way you can illustrate your point is to look online or ask around to find out about the nearest Senior Games. These are put together to resemble the Olympics, only for people who are more in the age group that would include grandparents. If you're ambitious, you could take your grandchildren and watch some of the events. It's good for grandchildren to understand that grandparents can be active, too! (They just might not have the stamina of youth.) You could even make a scrapbook about your Senior Olympics visit!

WHILE YOU'RE MAKING A SCRAPBOOK:

▶ Have your grandchildren describe their friends in as much detail as possible.

▶ Try to put something in the scrapbook about their parents.

▶ Be sure to print the title of the scrapbook on the front.

▶ If you run a pencil back and forth across a finger, your grandchild can put a fingerprint in the scrapbook. Cover it with tape so it won't wear off!

S
C
R
A
P
B
O
O
K

13

COMPUTER THINGS TO DO

▼

I F THERE'S ONE thing we can safely predict about the world our grand-children will be living in when they become adults, it's that there will be personal computers around. Computers will almost certainly be involved with their college education and their careers. The sooner you can introduce your grandchildren to computers, the better. Of course, the parents might already have this base covered. That's fine. But as we've learned, different people will bring different skills and perspectives to the table. The activities that you do on the computer might help your grandchildren's education by making them more proficient with computer use. It could make them more at ease in the digital world. All of these are good reasons to do these computer activities with your grandchildren. If you need to hone your own skills, there are plenty of adult classes available at community colleges and libraries. You could learn right along with your grandchildren! How's that for a great bonding process? There's an endless supply of activities to do on the computer, and we've included a few here that we believe will help you open up to your grandchildrens' world.

We'd like to remind you to also enjoy activities that require more physical exertion, so we suggest that not all of your time be spent online.

DID YOU KNOW?

We're all aware of the shysters who try to talk us out of our money, but there's a whole new breed on the Internet—and because they hide overseas and use fake computer references, they're difficult to track down. If the grandkids are old enough to be alone at the computer, you should go over Internet scams with them. They should never type their addresses or any other personal information in an email or on a website. Have a talk with the parents, too, and make sure everybody is on board with these precautions. It's best for them to know about the scams that are out there on the Internet before they fall prey to one. Many scams have attained urban legend status. That is, they've been around forever, relatively speaking, and they keep resurfacing. An excellent website to read about these is www. snopes.com. This website also covers scams. Let the grandchildren know that they shouldn't be alarmed, for example, when they get an email that says their personal information has been lost and they need to give their social security numbers. This is nearly always a scam; an attempt to steal identities. If people have your social security number and other information, they can get credit cards in your name—and you get the bills! If you have a question about whether a request for information is legitimate, find a telephone number for the business in question and call them.

MORE INFORMATION: BOOKS

Ford, Michael. *Scams and Scoundrels: Protect Yourself from the Dark Side of eBay and PayPal.* Elite Minds Inc. 2007.
A great beginner's book which covers all types of scams and methods to identify them.

Kirchheimer, Sid. *Scam-Proof Your Life: 377 Smart Ways to Protect You & Your Family from Ripoffs, Bogus Deals & Other Consumer Headaches.* Sterling. NY: 2007.

This book will leave readers well-informed on what to look for and what to do.

The Silver Lake Editors. *Scams & Swindles: Phishing, Spoofing, ID Theft, Nigerian Advance Schemes Investment Frauds: How to Recognize and Avoid Rip-Offs in the Internet Age.* Silver Lake Publishing. Lansdowne, PA: 2006.

The title says it all!

Vesper and Vesper. *100% Internet Credit Card Fraud Protected.* Trafford Publishing. Victoria, BC, Canada: 2006.

This book gives insight on credit card and identify theft, and how to protect yourself online.

More Information: Websites

www.scambusters.org

An excellent comprehensive list of scams on the Internet.

www.snopes.com

Reference site that covers urban legends, folklore, myths, rumors, and misinformation.

www.sec.gov/consumer/cyberfr.htm

Government site with great information about how to protect yourself from Internet fraud.

LYRICS

Fun Fact

The oldest recorded music notation, denoting both notes and words, is over 3,000 years old.

It's getting more and more difficult to understand the lyrics of songs on the radio and MTV these days. But even with the songs that were popular in our youth, we seldom knew *all* the words. Robin thought Creedence Clearwater Revival was singing, "There's a bathroom on the right." When it's time to log on, get the grandchildren together and decide on a popular song that you'd like to see the lyrics to. Look them up at www.lyricstop.com and lyrics.astraweb.com. You should be able to find what you're looking for at one of these. And if not, you can always type in the name of the song, add the word "lyrics," into Google and do a search. Once you have the lyrics, have your grandchildren sing the song to you. It's a good idea to take the lyrics after they're printed and read through them quickly by yourself so that the grandkids aren't exposed to words that are inappropriate. If your grandchildren are young, have them try to think of songs from Disney or other children's movies, as these will be safe. While you're at it, look up the lyrics to a song that you enjoyed when you were a teenager. How about that love song from your youth? See if the lyrics match your memory of the words.

A GRANDPARENTING ASIDE

If there's one thing we remember from when we were young, it's that we listened to the music that we liked, regardless of parental approval. There was some fairly suggestive language, especially in the songs of the rock and roll revolution. You're not going to be able to dictate what songs your grandchildren are listening to. However, you can certainly express your disapproval. And you certainly are under no obligation to have that music played in your house, or have those lyrics read aloud in your house. If your grandchildren are older, you can have a talk with them about how harmful and degrading some of the language is. This may have no effect on their listening habits, but it might get them to start thinking about their selections. Don't forget that you can offer alternatives. Introduce them to some of the music you enjoy. You might be surprised that they will enjoy it, too! (Some Beatles songs are being introduced to a fourth generation in our family.)

WHILE YOU'RE READING SONG LYRICS:

▶ Can you can write your own lyrics to a popular tune, replacing the words with your own?

▶ Have everybody vote for their favorite song lyrics of the day.

▶ Talk about the lyrics. What do the words mean? What kind of emotions are they portraying?

▶ Look up the lyrics to the Star-Spangled Banner.

EMAIL

If your grandchildren are older, they may already have their own email accounts. But if they're younger, and you have permission from the parents, help your grandchildren set up an email account and send their first email. Younger children need exposure to computers and their operation. You'll be helping them to become computer literate, and email accounts are very easy to set up. Yahoo is a popular site. Try visiting www.mail.yahoo.com and following the online directions for setting up a new account. Google also has a free webmail service at www.gmail.com, and there is Hotmail at www.hotmail.com. Have email addresses of relatives handy, so that after you set up an account for your grandchildren, you can help them send an email to family members. When they're getting started, you might need to help them with things to say. That's all right. Have your grandchildren tell everybody about their visit with you.

Some things to keep in mind:

▶ If they're younger, you'll want to write down the password somewhere because there's a strong chance they'll forget.

▶ If you have a digital camera, take a picture and have the grandchildren email the picture to family members.

▶ If your grandchildren are feeling creative, have them write a poem and email it to family members.

▶ Make sure your grandchildren understand that it's okay to send short emails at first. They'll gain confidence later and write longer ones.

A GRANDPARENTING ASIDE

Unfortunately, we've seen our share of family members and friends leave this earth for higher planes of existence in recent years. Regardless of religion, there have been some common reactions and that's been almost universal regret at not saying particular things before the opportunity to say them had passed. Mostly they involved the simple expression of love. The time with your grandchildren is precious. Make the most of it; express your feelings and love and compassion to them, and help them to express theirs to you. Don't hold grudges against their parents about how they are being raised. If your adult children have a grudge against you, ask them to get rid of it because our time on earth is too short for ill feelings. While some comedians say mockingly, "Can't we all just get along?" there's a certain amount of truth in trying to keep lines of communication open and always trying to strengthen our bonds between us. Hug your grandkids and their parents today and, indeed, whenever you see them.

WHILE YOU'RE SETTING UP
AN EMAIL ACCOUNT:

▶ Talk about how the letters you wrote when you were their age, and ask if they think emails will totally replace regular letters.

▶ Explain how regular mail sent through a post office is called "snail mail" because it moves, relative to the speed of an email, at a snail's pace.

▶ Ask if they can think of someone famous they would like to send an email to if they knew the email address. What would your grandchildren say in the email?

SIGNS

To make a sign, all you have to do is open a word processing program such as Microsoft Word. Select a large font (try "48"). Then, type in the words for your sign and print. If you have a color printer, you can try changing the colors of the text using the FORMAT > FONT menu. We've found that black works best for visibility. There are all kinds of signs that you can print. If you're having a yard sale, for example, you'll need signs to hang up around the neighborhood. This simple activity will help the grandchildren understand how to pare down the information to the basics: when, what, and where. Saturday the 25th at 8:00 am, a yard sale, at Grandma's and Grandpa's. Try making a sign for their bedroom door. We discourage DO NOT ENTER signs unless it's as a joke. If nothing else, make a sign for the refrigerator door, perhaps with a saying such as "A Trip of 1,000 Miles Begins with a Single Step."

A GRANDPARENT ASIDE

With the Internet age an age of abbreviation and improper grammar has begun. It's possible that this is because many are communicating via handheld devices such as the Blackberry. While everybody enjoys a good shortcut, not capitalizing the first letter in a complete sentence is just being lazy, and when it sneaks into email and other written communication (like schoolwork) it leads to poor communication and poor grades. We're not suggesting that you be 100% accurate, but it would be a good idea to teach your grandchildren to proofread their emails (and letters) before they're sent. It will help them in the long run. College admission tests don't go by Blackberry rules.

WHILE YOU'RE MAKING SIGNS:

▶ Tell them to look at bulletin boards—many grocery stores have them—and read some of the notices that are there.

▶ Go on a drive with the grandchildren and talk about the effectiveness or ineffectiveness of the signs you see.

▶ Make your sign with letters all capitalized and take a vote as to how it looks.

▶ Try different fonts. Have fun! How about inserting clip art?

YOUTUBE

The website www.youtube.com has grown extremely popular. It's a website where ordinary people post video clips for all to see. On the main webpage, you can select a category; we suggest "comedy." Everybody can use a good laugh these days, right? Browse through the clips and click on the ones that have high ratings. Each clip is on a 5-star rating, so if it's 4 or greater, the chances are that it's fairly entertaining. (You'll want to make sure that the clip has no warning about harsh language.) Some people spend many hours watching the clips, and more than a few have gone on to fame on network television. In any event, it's a fun activity, and you'll enjoy watching a few with your grandchildren. If you're brave and you have a digital recorder, you can make your own clip and upload it for all to see. See if your grandchildren have any ideas or interest in doing this.

A GRANDPARENT ASIDE

As your grandchildren get older, and if they are over at your house often (which we hope is the case), you might want to consider getting a second-hand computer for them. While we use our computer for many things, if your grandchildren are only using it for word processing, they don't need a latest-and-greatest model. Ask around and see what you can find secondhand. It's amazing how often our friends are updating their systems and are getting rid of old computers. It's a good idea to make sure there's nothing left on those computers that isn't meant for children's eyes, so if you know anybody who's good with computers (or can do it yourself), consider reformatting the hard drive and reinstalling the operating system. And while we're on the subject, it's always a good idea to back up your work. That is, if you have pictures on your hard drive, make sure you also have a copy of them on a CR-ROM or DVD disk. The same applies to written documents. It's the first lesson in working with computers, but it's also the one we all tend to forget (or ignore). So we'll say it one more time, back up your work!

WHILE YOU'RE VISITING YOUTUBE.COM:

▶ What's funny and what isn't in each video clip?

▶ Vote for a favorite clip of the day.

▶ Talk about a time in your life that you wish you could've recorded as a video clip. Do the grandchildren have any?

▶ Have everybody try to remember a part in their favorite movie that they'd like to see as a video clip.

SONG CLIPS

It's good to be involved with, or at least be aware of, the music in the lives of your grandchildren. And so when you're with them and are at the computer, considering browsing the Internet and listening to music clips. For the "Lyrics" activity, we suggested looking at the words. For this activity, find songs with instrumental segments that the grandchildren enjoy. Nowadays, most of the music that can be found in clip format is associated with videos, and you can find good selections at www.music.yahoo.com/musicvideos and www.findvideos.com. However, you can also find music clips at www.freeaudioclips.com. And if you're looking for something specific, you can always do a Google search for the title of the song and adding the words "music clip" in the search field. Recently, we watched a high school orchestra performance and heard a song that was excellent but that we weren't familiar with. Luckily we had brought home the flyer! So we did a Google search and found that we could listen to clips of the song from a CD that was on sale at www.amazon.com. It was great to hear the song again, and our music universe expanded. Try to do the same for your grandchildren.

A GRANDPARENT ASIDE

The Internet is a wide-open space where there's virtually no regulation. This poses a great danger to grandchildren. While we don't want to discourage grandchildren from exploring the world (indeed, we encourage it!), we do believe that it is the responsibility of parents and grandparents to help ensure they're kept safe during their explorations. We've already talked about how scammers can steal both your money and your virtual identity. But there are so many other dangers that haven't even appeared on the radar screen yet. Websites such as www.MySpace.com rise from obscurity and are extremely popular practically overnight. Keep aware of trends on the Internet, and think about the dangers that they might pose to innocent children. Learn how to filter content on the computers the grandchildren use, and make sure that parents know, too!

WHILE YOU'RE FINDING SONG CLIPS:

▶ Vote for the best song.

▶ Try different genres. If your grandchildren have never listened to classical music, give it a whirl.

▶ If you watch a music video, try closing your eyes and just listen. Ask your grandchildren if this helped them hear the notes better.

▶ Try to find a clip for one of your favorite songs from your youth.

LOCAL NEWS

Watching the six o'clock news used to be a national pastime. Many times this was done just after the evening meal. Local news stations are still in business, but it seems that much of the nation now gets its news via the Internet. Look for the call letters for your local news stations. If you do a Google search for those letters, you'll almost certainly find the website for your local news station. Sit down with your grandchildren and read through it together. Many times there will be a community calendar, which can show your grandchildren how much is happening in their area. Maybe they'll see something that interests them, such as a rodeo or a parade. Many stories are very interesting, just not of national interest, so you'll rarely see them on CNN.

A GRANDPARENT ASIDE

One of the greatest gifts you can give your grandchildren is a feeling of worth and usefulness. Isn't that true for adults, too? Don't we all want to feel like we're having an effect on this planet? Give your grandchildren an assignment to help you keep up to date on computers and technology. When they're young, you'll be the ones showing them how to do most things, but believe us when we say that they'll be on to new technologies with which you're unfamiliar in the blink of an eye. We were just getting to the point of switching all of our music over from cassettes and vinyl albums to CD-ROM when MP-3 players came along. Now we're thinking that we need to store everything on a hard drive. This is just one example of a trend; kids will be more up to date on the latest technologies because their peers will keep them informed. So have them explain it to you! Have them help you to hook up the latest peripheral device to your computer. If they're younger, they won't know how. But tell them there'll come a day when it's something you hope they'll help you with.

WHILE YOU'RE AT THE LOCAL NEWS WEBSITE:

▶ Have your grandchildren ask their teachers to talk about an important local news story. Discuss their responses with your grandchildren.

▶ Can they explain the weather icons, such as a cloud partially blocking a sun, when the weather section comes on? Why did the news show choose that icon?

▶ Ask them, before the news comes on, to pick out their favorite news story. Talk about why they chose that particular story.

▶ Would they like to see anything local (such as an event at their school) covered by the news station?

QUESTION & ANSWER

We were wondering once: what's written on the slab of stone in Rockefeller Center in New York City? After some thought about which words to put into the Google search engine, we typed them in and there was our answer! It's amazing how much information is out there on the Internet. Accessing that information through the correct keywords is the trick. While we enjoy using Google, there are other search engines you can use such as Ask.com and Yahoo. Use the one that you're most comfortable with. Get your grandchildren together and start wondering aloud about things. How did the world get to be the way it is? What happened to the dinosaurs? How far is Timbuktu? Is there such a thing as an albino penguin? Your grandchildren should be great at coming up with these off-beat questions. Start with a list of several questions of your own. That way, if you happen to be unsuccessful with a search, you can move on to the next question. This teaches your grandchildren how to access information, and since we're living in an information age, it's a valuable skill that will help them tremendously as they prepare for adulthood.

A GRANDPARENTING ASIDE

It wouldn't come as a surprise to us if you get negative feedback at some point from the parents about how you help expand the universe of the grandchildren. Parents are the ones who are responsible for the kids, and they have a perfect right to raise issues with you as to what their children are exposed to. That's fine. Take their points seriously and respond rationally. We are trying to widen the grandchildren's horizons and to open their eyes to what's out there in the real world. They won't be under the parents' umbrella forever—the sooner they start down on the road to independence, the better. It might be that it's the independence part of the equation that frightens parents. After all, these are their babies! As grandparents, you'll probably be able to spot their growth much more quickly than the parents. It can be difficult for parents to let go and to allow the fledglings to leave the nest. Understand their concern, acknowledge it, and move on.

WHILE YOU'RE SEARCHING FOR INFORMATION:

▶ Search for any famous names your grandchildren know. Talk about why they know that name. Where did they hear the name?

▶ Try to have your grandchildren think of the name of a country. Do a search and read about it. Talk about how it differs from the United States.

▶ Have everyone come up with one historical event to do a search for. Ask why they chose that particular event.

▶ Do a search for the school that the grandchildren attend and see if it has a website. See if your grandchildren can explain why or why not the website is an accurate portrayal of the school.

DICTIONARY

We can all remember when we were in grade school and asked our teacher what a word meant and the teacher would tell us to look it up in a dictionary. What was worse was when we asked how a word was spelled and the teacher said the same thing. How could we look it up if we didn't know how to spell it? You might have the same problem with online dictionaries, but at least you can quickly enter several variations of spelling until you get it right. Many search engines and word processing programs will also prompt you when you misspell a word and will give you a spelling. Be careful; if you're really off, they might be suggesting the correct spelling of another word entirely! In any case, it's a good idea to introduce your grandchildren to the world of online dictionaries. This will help increase their vocabulary to communicate in a world that places increasingly high values on communications skills. You can find the Merriam-Webster online dictionary at www.m-w.com. Other popular dictionary websites are www.dictionary.reference.com and www.dictionary.msn.com. Some websites, such as www.yourdictionary.com, are compilations of websites and offer translation services for other languages. Some of these sites have "Words of the Day," where you'll be introduced to words you didn't know before. Have your grandchildren use those in a sentence!

A GRANDPARENTING ASIDE

You've probably heard this before, but—the world is shrinking. Trips that once took days can now be done in hours by plane. You can find out what's going on anywhere in the world with a click of your mouse and a Google search. Events that take place in the far reaches of the globe have instant impacts on our lives. You can talk with anyone, no matter where they are, as long as there's a cell tower nearby. Keep this in mind if you frown upon the latest technologies or the newest gadgets, and talk about how unnecessary they are. They might be, but technology will continue to advance nonetheless. If your grandchildren don't keep up with it, they could be left behind. We were somewhat surprised when we discovered that many universities now require incoming freshmen to have laptop computers. Can you imagine how much of a disadvantage a student would have if their parents were computer illiterate? Keep up with the advances in technology as best you can, and if something new comes along, have your grandchildren explain it to you. Odds are they'll know all about it. And if they don't, they can probably find out for you.

WHILE YOU'RE AT A DICTIONARY WEBSITE:

▶ If you're learning a new word, it often helps to retain the knowledge by writing the word with pen and paper and then using it in a sentence.

▶ Do they know what a thesaurus is? Find a new word using one.

- ▶ Ask them to find a word and then ask you if you know the meaning.
- ▶ Do they know how to use phonetic symbols? Those are the marks that help you to pronounce the words correctly. Look up a site online that will teach them how.

PRODUCT EVALUATION

Fun Fact

In 1965, Ralph Nader released *Unsafe at Any Speed,* a study that purported to demonstrate the unsafe engineering of many American automobiles.

Introduce your grandchildren to the world of consumer reviews. Pretend that you're going to make a purchase; anything from an automobile to a refrigerator. How can you know you're getting the best bang for your buck? How do you know you're not buying a lemon? What can you do to make sure you're not ripped off? Tell your grandkids about the many websites out there where consumers provide feedback on the products they've purchased. The magazine *Consumer Reports* is a well-known resource. Check out www.consumerreports.org. You can get free samples of the kind of reports available, although there's a subscription fee for more detailed information. Other websites include www.consumersearch.com and www.ratings.net. For technology products, we've found a good website for reviews: www.cnet.com. Read through those reviews with your grandchildren and let them know what you think about your pretend purchase and why you'll feel better about it because you've done your homework. As a final note, it's always a good idea to check out those recalled toy products. Many recalls are issued because of safety hazards. Check out www.cpsc.gov/cpscpub/prerel/category/toy.html.

A GRANDPARENT ASIDE

Often it seems like so long since we've been children, we forget what it's like. Many of the things that we take for granted are entirely new to children. Remember being afraid to open a closet door? It's silly, right? But not to children. Let's hope we don't forget that we were once frightened by simple things, too. On the other side of the equation, children often take delight in the things we take for granted. The rain can mesmerize them, or an ant. They can teach us a thing or two sometimes. After all, it's the children who slow down and smell the roses. For them, it's a breathtaking moment. Take a cue from your grandchildren, slow down, and see the world through their eyes.

WHILE YOU'RE AT
A PRODUCT EVALUATION WEBSITE:

▶ Have your grandchildren tell you a product they want to look at. How about a big TV? Ask them to explain the reason for their choice.

▶ Check out the safety aspects of automobiles. Ask your grandchildren to explain why safety features are important when considering a purchase.

▶ For appliances, investigate energy usage. Why is it important? See if they understand how a more expensive product might be cheaper in the long run because it uses less electricity, which you pay for monthly via electric bills.

▶ Talk about safety recalls for toys. See if they can explain how toys can be dangerous if not properly manufactured.

CONCLUSION

▼

WE HEARD THAT the first of the Baby Boomers has officially "retired"—at least as far as the Social Security Administration is concerned. Because of Boomers, the image of grandparenting today is much different than in previous generations. Before us, it felt like grandparents stayed at home, cooked apple pies, and generally waited around in their rocking chairs for the grandkids to come and visit.

Today's grandparents are much more active. Many are still in the work force. We hope these active grandparents spend some of their time doing activities with their grandchildren. There will never again be a generation that grew up without cell phones, remote controls, and the Internet. Grandparents have a special opportunity to relate their unique experiences and wisdom to their grandchildren. We hope this book will spark some ideas on how to accomplish that. It's a great gift that grandparents can give to their grandchildren—their time. And what better way to spend time than having fun? Have fun grandparenting, and your grandchildren will be the wiser for it.

—Doug and Robin Hewitt

INDEX OF ACTIVITIES